sex

RACHEL WRIGHT

Additional material supplied by
Bobbi Whitcombe

Cover illustration by
David Scutt

Inside illustrations by
James Cotton

■ SCHOLASTIC

For Jude

Scholastic Children's Books,
Commonwealth House, 1-19 New Oxford Street,
London WC1A 1NU, UK
a division of Scholastic Ltd
London ~ New York ~ Toronto ~ Sydney ~ Auckland

First published by Scholastic Ltd, 1998

Text copyright © Rachel Wright, 1998
Cover illustration copyright © David Scutt, 1998
Inside illustrations © James Cotton, 1998

ISBN 0 590 19754 1

Typeset by TW Typesetting, Midsomer Norton, Avon
Printed by Cox & Wyman Ltd, Reading, Berks.

10 9 8 7 6 5 4 3 2 1

The right of Rachel Wright, David Scutt and James Cotton to be identified as
the author and illustrators of this work respectively has been asserted by them in
accordance with the Copyright, Designs and Patents Act, 1988.

ACKNOWLEDGEMENTS

The author and publishers would like to thank the following for their invaluable help and support: Brook Advisory Centres, the Family Planning Association, Marian Nicholson of the Herpes Viruses Association, Lothian Gay and Lesbian Switchboard, LRC Products Ltd, Gracia McGrath, Elizabeth Sacre, William and Edward Stevens, The Terrence Higgins Trust. We are also grateful to all the organizations who sent information (many of whom are listed in the back of this book).

Thanks are also due to Bobbi Whitcombe, for researching individual accounts; to Claire Chapman and Lynn Sutcliffe of the Pink Project, organized by the Spare Tyre Theatre Company; and to all those courageous young people who have been willing to share their very private experiences with us for the benefit of others.

Contraceptive information reproduced with permission of the Family Planning Association.

All medical information in this book is based on the evidence and medical opinion available at the time of writing.

Contents

Introduction

This book is for teenagers who want helpful information about the physical and emotional sides of sex, as well as pregnancy, birth control and sexual health. It doesn't suggest that you should be having sex in your teens – in fact it's against the law in Great Britain for a lad to have sexual intercourse with a girl who is under 16, and for two lads to have sex together before they are both 18. However, it does tell you things you need to know before you begin your first sexual relationship, as well as things you may want to know once that relationship has started. So, if you are thinking of starting a sexual relationship and want to know whether you are ready to take such a big step; or if you are already having a sexual relationship and have some questions you want answered; or even if you are nowhere near ready to have sex but just want to know what the whole business is about, chances are this book will tell you exactly what you want to know.

But before you get stuck into all the information inside, test your sex knowledge with the quiz on page 13. Keep a record of your answers, then try the quiz again when you've finished reading the book. Check both sets of your answers against those on page 180 and compare your two scores. The difference between your scores may take you by surprise.

Chapter 1

sex

PUBERTY AND PRIVATE PARTS

The sex facts challenge

Take note, some questions have more than one correct answer.

1. **A lad's testicles, or balls, hang outside his body because:**
a) the sperm inside his testicles need to be kept cooler than his main body temperature;
b) the sperm inside his testicles need to be kept away from his bladder in case they seep into his urine;
c) the arrangement of the male's sex tackle is a complete mystery.

2. **The external sexual organs that lie between a girl's legs are known as:**
a) the valva;
b) the vulva;
c) the volvo.

3. **If a lad masturbates, or rubs his private parts for pleasure, more than twice a week during his teens:**
a) he'll use up all his sperm before he's 20;
b) he'll use up all his sperm before he's 40;
c) he'll do himself no harm at all.

4. **When a lad ejaculates, or 'comes', he squirts out of his penis, on average:**
a) about one teaspoonful of semen;
b) about one dessertspoonful of semen;
c) about one tablespoonful of semen.

5. **A girl can become pregnant if:**
a) she has sex standing up;
b) she has sex during her period;
c) she washes out her vagina with water immediately after sex.

6. **Sperm can live inside a girl's body for up to:**
a) several minutes;
b) several hours;
c) several days.

7. To help prevent pregnancy, emergency contraceptive pills have to be taken:

a) the morning after having unprotected sex;

b) within 72 hours of having unprotected sex;

c) within five days of having unprotected sex.

8. A doctor can give contraception to a girl under 16 if:

a) she seems mature enough to understand the benefits and risks of the treatment given;

b) she brings a note from her parents;

c) she agrees not to use the contraceptives given until she is 16.

9. If a lad gets very excited sexually and then doesn't ejaculate, his testicles will:

a) feel uncomfortable for a bit;

b) shrivel up and stop making sperm;

c) turn blue and explode.

10. The best way to lessen the risk of catching HIV through vaginal sex is to:

a) keep the number of sexual partners you have to a minimum;

b) use a condom every time you have vaginal sex;

c) make sure the penis is pulled out of the vagina before ejaculation takes place.

11. The proper name for sucking and licking a penis is:

a) fellatio;

b) horatio;

c) cunnilingus.

12. Anal intercourse, or penis-to-bottom sex, is only legal if:

a) both partners are aged 16 or over;

b) both partners are aged 18 or over;

c) both partners have their parents' permission in writing.

Puberty: the low-down

During childhood girls' and boys' bodies look fairly alike. Then puberty, or sexual development, strikes and WHAM! Boys' shoulders and chests get broader and their penises get bigger; girls' hips and breasts get rounder and they begin having periods; and both sexes start sprouting hair in saucy places.

In this chapter you'll find a run-down of the physical changes that happen at puberty and a look at how your sex organs work. Even if you're sure you know all you need to know about puberty and your privates, have a read. Many fully-grown men and women have no idea of how their sexual bits work, let alone how their lover's sexual bits function. This is a shame because the more you know about how male and female bodies work, the more clued-up you'll be when you come to have sex.

Puberty can start at any time between the ages of 10 and 18 and can carry on into your late teens or early 20s. Usually, however, these changes start at around 12 or 13 for girls and 13 or 14 for boys. At the end of the day, it doesn't matter when you start or finish puberty. It makes no difference to what you'll be like as a full-grown adult.

Puberty can be a weird time if you don't know what to expect. Here's a quick canter through the main physical changes that happen at the start of puberty and later on.

Males

▶ Your shoulders widen.

▶ You get taller, heavier, stronger and more muscular.

▶ Your voice deepens. It may squeak and croak for a bit before it hits its new lower range: this is normal.

▶ Your penis and testicles get bigger.

▶ Your testicles start to produce sperm.

▶ You start to get erections, or hard-ons, more often.

▶ You grow lots more hair on different parts of your body, such as on and under your arms, on your legs, face and chest and around your penis and testicles, or genitals. Just for the record, some lads never grow chest hair and facial hair is one of the last things to appear.

▶ Your nipples can be a bit sensitive and you may get extra pads of fat behind them for a while.

▶ Your joints may ache for a bit.

▶ Blackheads and spots may appear on your face, neck, chest and back, and your hair may get greasier. If your spots get really bad, you may need to see your doctor.

▶ You start to sweat more and the sweat smells more strongly than it used to. The sweat glands that develop around puberty are scent glands. They give you your own sexy smell. You only start to smell bad when the sweat is left on your skin for too long.

16

Females

▶ You grow breasts and your nipples get bigger. Both may feel slightly tender as they grow, so try to avoid getting bashed in the chest!

▶ Your hips get rounder.

▶ You get taller and stronger.

▶ You get heavier. This doesn't mean you'll end up fat!

▶ You may get greasy skin, hair and spots.

▶ You sweat a bit more and the sweat smells stronger (see the note about sweat above).

▶ Your voice sounds slightly lower and deeper, although you may not notice this as it happens.

▶ Hair starts growing more thickly around your private parts, or genitals, under your arms and on your arms and legs.

▶ You may grow a bit of hair around your nipples, near your belly button or around your chin and upper lip.

▶ You start having periods. Most girls start between the ages of 10 and 16.

A nether regions tour of the male body

Penis
aka (also known as)

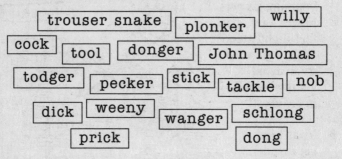

trouser snake · plonker · willy · cock · tool · donger · John Thomas · todger · pecker · stick · tackle · nob · dick · weeny · wanger · schlong · prick · dong

If you are the proud owner of a penis you probably already know that it has two main parts, the head and the shaft. As you've no doubt discovered, the head is more sensitive than the shaft, particularly around the rim, and the ridge of skin on the underside, where the head joins the shaft, is also super sensitive. The loose fold of skin that covers the head of your penis when it is soft is called the foreskin. When you get an erection, or hard-on, your foreskin pulls back and the head of your penis is exposed.

You should be able to move your foreskin back and forth easily over the head of your penis. If it is tight, you could try and ease it back gently either in the bath using some soap, or on dry land using some non-water based lubricant (see page 113). In time this may stretch the foreskin enough to enable it to move more easily. If this doesn't work, have a chat with your doctor. S/he may suggest a small operation to loosen your foreskin.

Talking of foreskins and soap, it is important to wash under your foreskin once a day. If you don't, a yellowish-white goo called smegma will build up which can smell unpleasant and cause soreness. More importantly, build-ups of smegma have been linked with cancer of the penis in later life.

18

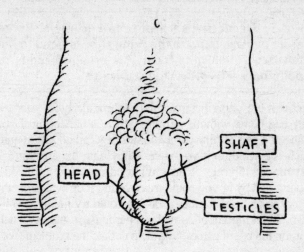

Circumcision

Not all males have foreskins. A few are born without one and many more have theirs removed, usually for religious reasons. Removal of the foreskin is called circumcision. It doesn't affect a man's ability to enjoy sex or masturbation in the slightest.

Erections
aka (also known as)

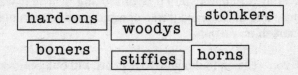

Your penis is made of spongy tissue full of blood vessels. When you get sexually excited, or sometimes for no obvious reason at all, extra blood pumps into your penis and this makes it become erect, i.e. grow longer and wider and stick upwards from your body stiffly. When the excitement goes away, the extra blood drains away and your penis shrinks back to its normal size.

19

> **FACT:** Erections vary from male to male. Some erect penises bend to the right. Others bend to the left. As a man gets older, his erection tends to point outwards rather than upwards.

Erections are unpredictable things, particularly in your teens. They can come without warning which is unnerving if you're posing in a pair of flimsy trunks. And they can go just as quickly which is a wind-up if you were happy with the erection in the first place. If you get an unwanted erection and you are embarrassed by it, you could try covering it up with something, such as your hands or a bag, or you could try gently pushing it down. Thinking about something particularly unsexy, such as your top ten board games, may help deflate the problem too.

Size matters
As lads who use locker rooms know, penis sizes vary. However, during an erection a small soft penis generally grows more than a large soft penis, so the difference in length is not very great. If you are hung up about the size of your penis, here are a few other things to bear in mind:

▶ Your penis usually shrinks when you're feeling worried or cold, so unless you've been looking at it in a warm place and in a relaxed frame of mind, you've been doing yourself no favours.

▶ If you've been looking at your penis without a mirror, it will seem smaller to you than it does to others because you are looking down at it.

▶ And finally ... who cares how big or small your penis is? Penis size has nothing to do with how good a lover you will be. Besides, most women are less interested in the size of their lover's penis and more interested in the size of his wit, warmth and confidence.

> **FACT:** On average, a fully-grown, adult penis is about 8.5 cm to 10.5 cm long when soft and about 12.5 cm to 17.5 cm long when fully erect.

The truth about testicles
aka (also known as)

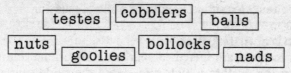

Just behind your penis you have two egg-shaped balls hanging in a bag of skin called the scrotum, or ball-bag. Each ball or testicle should be about the same size and weight as the other, but don't be alarmed if one, usually the left, hangs slightly lower than the other. This clever arrangement helps stop your testicles from crushing or bashing into each other when you ride a bicycle or go for a run.

After puberty, your scrotum is usually hairy and darker than your normal skin colour. When it is warm and you're feeling relaxed, it is smooth and soft and hangs right down. When it is cold or you're feeling tense or sexy, your scrotum scrunches up towards your body and its skin becomes tighter. It does this either to keep your testicles warm or to protect them from physical damage.

Why do testicles dangle?
You may think it crazy that something as delicate as your testicles should be left dangling on the outside of your body, unprotected from any boot or blow coming their way. Yet there is a good reason for this. The tiny tadpole-shaped sperm that are needed to join with a girl's egg to start a baby are made in your testicles and in order to work properly, the sperm must be kept cooler than your main body temperature. So your sperm-filled testicles hang outside your body where the air can reach them and keep them cool.

FACT: Research has shown that Finnish men have healthier sperm than other men. Why this should be, no one is sure, but one factor may be that up until 1980 mothers in Finland were much less likely to smoke than mothers in other parts of Europe, and smoking whilst pregnant can affect the testicles of a developing male foetus.

Coming and going

Your testicles are linked to your penis by a long thin tube called the urethra which runs down the middle of your penis and opens out at the tip. Both urine, or pee, and semen, or spunk, pass down this tube on their way out of your body. They never come out at the same time though

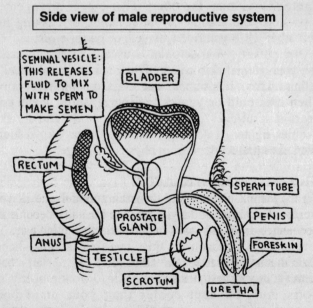

Side view of male reproductive system

SEMINAL VESICLE: THIS RELEASES FLUID TO MIX WITH SPERM TO MAKE SEMEN

BLADDER

RECTUM

SPERM TUBE

PROSTATE GLAND

PENIS

ANUS

FORESKIN

TESTICLE

SCROTUM

URETHA

because whenever your penis is erect and ready to shoot out some semen, a little valve closes off your bladder.

Semen
aka (also known as)

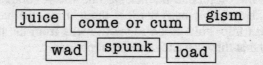

Semen is a milky liquid which contains millions of sperm. Sometimes semen is thin and watery. At other times it is quite thick. It stays inside your body until you get so sexually excited that you can no longer hold it in. Then it comes spurting out of the end of your penis in short bursts. This is called ejaculating.

Ejaculating
aka (also known as)

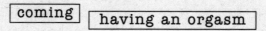

The average ejaculation produces about one teaspoonful of semen. This teaspoonful can contain as many as 600 million sperm. It only takes one sperm to join with a girl's egg to start a baby.

Wet dreams
At some time or other, most lads who are sexually developed wake up to find that they have 'come' in their sleep. Night-time ejaculations like these are sometimes called wet dreams. They are perfectly normal and usually become less frequent once the lad starts to masturbate or to have sex.

Pubic hair (male and female)
aka (also known as)

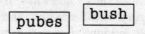

23

The hair that grows on and around your private parts at puberty is called pubic hair. At first it is soft and fine, then it becomes coarser and thicker. No one knows for sure why humans have pubic hair, but it is thought that the hair acts as a scent trap, holding on to sexy smells from the private parts so that they can excite a sexual partner.

A nether regions tour of the female body

If you're a girl the following information about your external sex organs, or vulva, will make more sense if you look at yourself with a mirror while you read the text. Find somewhere well-lit where you can be private. Wash your hands. Then sit on the floor with your legs wide apart and your knees bent. Place the mirror so that you can see between your legs and prop this book up next to you.

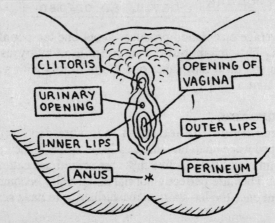

Vaginal lips

The first thing you'll probably notice when you take a look at your vulva is a pair of fleshy outer lips. If you gently part these with your fingers, you'll see two inner lips which are hairless. These outer and inner lips vary from girl to girl so don't worry if yours don't look exactly like those in magazines or textbooks.

Clitoris
aka (also known as)

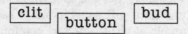

Just above the spot where your inner lips meet, you'll find a little bump about the size of a small pea. This is your clitoris. You may need to pull back the fold of skin covering your clitoris to see it more clearly. The clitoris is the female equivalent to the penis. If you gently press, touch or stroke the bit you can see, or the ridge under the skin just above it, you should get a delicious feeling.

Below your clitoris you'll find a tiny slit or opening – keep looking, it's there somewhere! This is the opening of your urethra. Your urethra is the short tube through which urine, or pee, passes when you go to the toilet.

Vagina on view
aka (also known as)

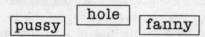

Below your 'pee-hole' you'll see a larger opening. This is the opening of your vagina. Around the opening to your vagina, or even partly blocking it, you may be able to see a thin stretchy fold of skin called the hymen. Some girls are born without a hymen. Others stretch and break theirs without knowing it when they run about, ride a bike, use a tampon or have sex.

> In days gone by people thought that you could tell a girl was a virgin if her hymen was unbroken. They were wrong!

25

Your vagina is a tube about 7.5 to 10 centimetres long. It runs from your uterus, or womb, to the outside of your body. When you have a period, blood travels from your uterus and out through your vagina. If/when you have vaginal sex, sperm from your partner's penis travels the other way. The walls of your vagina are soft and stretchy. In fact, they are so stretchy they can let a stiff penis in and a baby's head out without any trouble at all. If you feel comfortable with the idea, wash your hands and gently slide your middle finger into your vagina. Make sure its nail is short. (If you have an intact hymen you probably won't be able to insert your finger more than a few centimetres.) Push very gently around the walls of the vagina and feel its softness for yourself. Now gently slide your finger up your vagina, at an angle towards the small of your back. If you push your finger up high enough you should be able to touch something that feels like a nose with a small dimple in it. This is your cervix*. The 'dimple' is a hole which leads into your uterus. Although it can widen enough to let a baby out, it won't let a finger, penis or tampon in.

A look inside

Obviously you can't have a good rummage around your uterus and ovaries, like you can your vagina. However, if you put your thumbs and forefingers together to form a triangle, and then put the tips of your forefingers on the bone just above where your legs meet, you'll get a rough idea of where your uterus and ovaries are in your body.

Uterus (aka womb) and ovaries

Your uterus, once it is fully-grown, is about the size of your fist. Attached to the upper end of it, on either side, are two tubes called Fallopian tubes. At the end of each tube is a small almond-shaped organ called an ovary. Each ovary contains thousands of immature ova or eggs.

---

* If you can't find your cervix, lie flat on your back, pull your knees up to your chest and try again.

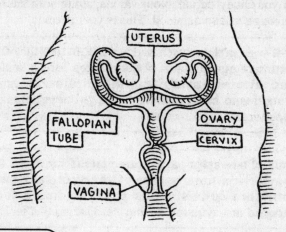

Front view of female reproductive system

UTERUS

FALLOPIAN TUBE

OVARY

CERVIX

VAGINA

Periods

aka (also known as)

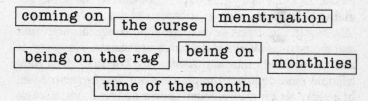

coming on

the curse

menstruation

being on the rag

being on

monthlies

time of the month

At some point during puberty your ovaries step up a gear and each month one of them releases a mature ovum, or egg. This is called ovulation. At about the same time, the lining of your uterus begins to thicken, ready for a possible pregnancy. Once the egg has been released, it moves along a Fallopian tube towards your uterus. If sperm gets into your vagina shortly before or while the egg is in this tube, one of the sperm may swim up and join with, or fertilize, the egg. If this happens, the fertilized egg will attach itself to the lining of your uterus and grow into a baby. (See page

103 for more about how pregnancy happens.) If the travelling egg doesn't meet a sperm, it breaks up and passes out of your body through your vagina, along with the extra uterus lining and some blood. This is your period.

> **FACT:** A girl is born with 40,000 to 400,000 immature eggs in each of her ovaries. Unlike a lad who starts making sperm at puberty and continues to make it all his life, a girl never makes any more eggs.

> **FACT:** On average, a girl has periods for 30 to 40 years. This means that of the thousands of immature eggs she has at birth, only a few hundred are ovulated during her lifetime.

Menstrual merry-go-round

The time between the start of one period and the day before the start of the next is called the menstrual cycle. A menstrual cycle lasting 28 days is considered the norm, but many girls have cycles which are shorter or longer than this. For the first year or two, the time between one period and the next can vary, so if you've just started your periods and they're irregular and scanty, don't worry. Once they become more regular, it might be worth noting them down in a diary or on the calendar shown opposite. Put a cross through each day that you bleed. After a few months you'll be able to see when your next period is likely to start and how long it will last.

Sanitary pads v tampons

A period can last from about two to eight days and girls use either tampons or sanitary pads during this time to soak up the blood. Both sanitary pads and tampons can be bought from chemists, supermarkets and local foodstores. Even if you haven't started your periods yet, it might be worth

Your monthly check-up!

Dec 15	12	9	9	6	4	Jun 1	29	27	24	21	19	16	14
16	13	10	10	7	5	2	30	28	25	22	20	17	15
17	14	11	11	8	6	3	Jul 1	29	26	23	21	18	16
18	15	12	12	9	7	4	2	30	27	24	22	19	17
19	16	13	13	10	8	5	3	31	28	25	23	20	18
20	17	14	14	11	9	6	4	Aug 1	29	26	24	21	19
21	18	15	15	12	10	7	5	2	30	27	25	22	20
22	19	16	16	13	11	8	6	3	31	28	26	23	21
23	20	17	17	14	12	9	7	4	Sep 1	29	27	24	22
24	21	18	18	15	13	10	8	5	2	30	28	25	23
25	22	19	19	16	14	11	9	6	3	Oct 1	29	26	24
26	23	20	20	17	15	12	10	7	4	2	30	27	25
27	24	21	21	18	16	13	11	8	5	3	31	28	26
28	25	22	22	19	17	14	12	9	6	4	Nov 1	29	27
29	26	23	23	20	18	15	13	10	7	5	2	30	28
30	27	24	24	21	19	16	14	11	8	6	3	Dec 1	29
31	28	25	25	22	20	17	15	12	9	7	4	2	30
Jan 1	29	26	26	23	21	18	16	13	10	8	5	3	31
2	30	27	27	24	22	19	17	14	11	9	6	4	Jan 1
3	31	28	28	25	23	20	18	15	12	10	7	5	2
4	Feb 1	Mar 1	29	26	24	21	19	16	13	11	8	6	3
5	2	2	30	27	25	22	20	17	14	12	9	7	4
6	3	3	31	28	26	23	21	18	15	13	10	8	5
7	4	4	Apr 1	29	27	24	22	19	16	14	11	9	6
8	5	5	2	30	28	25	23	20	17	15	12	10	7
9	6	6	3	May 1	29	26	24	21	18	16	13	11	8
10	7	7	4	2	30	27	25	22	19	17	14	12	9
11	8	8	5	3	31	28	26	23	20	18	15	13	10

Adapted from *The Women Artists Diary 1998*, published by The Women's Press keeping some pads or tampons at home and in your bag, for when you need them.

Sanitary pads are long, soft pads which you wear inside your knickers. They work by soaking up the blood as it leaves your vagina. They come in different thicknesses and the idea is you use the thicker pads when the flow is heavy and the thinner towels when the flow is light. The best way to get rid of a used pad is to put it in a bag and throw it in a bin. You should not dispose of pads or tampons down the toilet unless their packaging says they are fully flushable.

Advantages They are easy to use; you can see when one needs changing; most have a plastic backing to stop any blood leaking through; ideal to wear on those days when you think your period may start.

Disadvantages They can feel a bit bulky; they sometimes slip; you can't wear one in water.

Tampons are short compact rolls of cotton wool with a string attached to one end. The idea is that you push a tampon up into your vagina and leave it there to soak up the blood. When you're ready to change the tampon you pull the string, which hangs outside your body, and throw the tampon away. You must change your tampons fairly frequently (see the instruction booklet in each packet) and you must always remove a used tampon before you put a new one in. Like sanitary pads, tampons come in different thicknesses. Some also come with a pair of cardboard tubes on the outside, to help you put the tampon in.

Advantages They're comfortable to wear; they don't take up much space in your bag; you can wear one swimming.

Disadvantages It can be difficult to know when to change one; it can take time to learn how to use one; not great if you want to have a lie-in (if used overnight, tampons must be changed after eight hours); can cause infection if you put one in with dirty fingers. Tampon use has been linked to a rare condition called Toxic Shock Syndrome.

Tampon trouble

Toxic Shock Syndrome, or TSS for short, is a very rare but serious type of blood poisoning which is caused by common bacteria. Anyone can get TSS but half of reported cases seem to be linked to women using tampons. People suffering from TSS tend to feel very ill, very quickly, and need immediate medical treatment. The symptoms to look out for are: sudden high temperature (usually about 39°C or higher), diarrhoea, vomiting, a sunburn-like rash, a sore throat, muscle aches, feeling faint or actually fainting. If you develop two or more of these symptoms remove your tampon (if you're wearing one) and see a doctor immediately. Remember to tell him/her that you have been using tampons. Although the link between tampons and TSS is not clear, experts think that the risk of TSS can be reduced if you always use the lowest absorbency tampon for your flow and you use a sanitary pad from time to time during your period.

Tampons for beginners

Every packet of tampons comes with an instruction leaflet which you should read, even if you are an experienced tampon-user, as the information is updated from time to time. However, if you're new to tampons, here's some additional information you may find helpful or interesting:

▶ Learning to use a tampon can take time, so be patient.

▶ It's best to practise using a tampon during your period. Wearing a tampon when you're not bleeding can cause soreness and dryness.

▶ Slender or mini tampons are the easiest to insert.

▶ If you can feel a tampon once it is inside you, you probably haven't pushed it in far enough.

▶ Using a tampon doesn't affect your virginity. You are a virgin until you have sexual intercourse.

▶ You can't lose a tampon inside you as there's nowhere for it to go (see page 26).

▶ If you push the cord up inside you by mistake, squat down, strain hard as though you were pushing something out of your vagina and pull the tampon out with your thumb and first finger. Make sure they are clean! If this doesn't work ask your mum or doctor to help. Doctors are used to rescuing things far weirder than tampons from inside people's bodies, so don't be embarrassed.

Period problems

Some girls sail through their periods without so much as a twinge. Others suffer from all sorts of discomfort either before or during their period. Feeling foul before your period is known as Premenstrual Syndrome or Premenstrual Tension – PMS or PMT for short. Common PMS symptoms include constipation, diarrhoea, sore breasts, spots, bloatedness, sluggishness, irritability and depression. Common ills that occur during a period are back-ache, belly cramps and feeling sick. Sadly there is no single sure-fire remedy guaranteed to cure all period pains. However, if you find your periods heavy going, the following self-help remedies may be of use.

Bellyaches and back-aches If you suffer from either of these, you could try doing one or more of the following: holding a hot water bottle against the part that hurts; taking a painkiller designed for period cramps; massaging your back and belly; having a hot bath; going for a swim; going for a walk, doing yoga or some other type of relaxing exercise.

Food Eating a well-balanced diet, which includes fresh fruit and vegetables, makes sense whatever kind of periods you have, but eating more fresh fruit, vegetables and whole grains in the week before your period can help with constipation. You may also find that a diet which keeps your blood sugar up at a steady level – in other words, eating small frequent meals which contain high fibre, low sugar, starchy foods, throughout the day – can help reduce PMS problems. Try cutting out added salt and sugar, alcohol and caffeine (which is found in tea, coffee and some soft drinks) for at least the week before your period, too.

Some women who suffer from PMS find it helps to increase their intake of vitamin B6. B6 can be found in brewer's yeast, wheat germ, wheat bran, whole grains, pulses, cabbage, liver, kidney and eggs. This vitamin is also available in pill form from health food shops. However, current Government thinking suggests that you should not take a daily dose of more than 10 milligrams of vitamin B6 in the form of dietary supplements, unless prescribed by a doctor, as high levels of this vitamin over a prolonged period of time may cause harmful side-effects.

Depression and irritability If you think that you suffer from premenstrual depression, you might find it helpful to start keeping a record of how you feel before and during each period. That way you'll soon be able to work out which days you are likely to feel down. When you've identified your 'down' days, you can plan ahead and try to arrange treats for yourself or avoid doing stressful things during that time. If you find that you get tired during these days, you can also set aside more time for sleep or relaxation.

These are not the only self-help remedies available and you may find that your mum, older sister or girlfriends have other tried-and-tested remedies which work better for you. If, however, none of these suggestions helps, have a chat with your doctor or a qualified alternative practitioner such as a homeopath. You may find that they can sort you out. There is also a National Society for Premenstrual Syndrome which offers a support telephone line for PMS sufferers (see page 190 for details).

My periods were fairly normal until I was about 14. I'd started to become interested in boys around then. Then they became quite irregular and I didn't have one at all for about a year and a half. I was quite worried and even wondered if I might be pregnant, but I wasn't. I didn't want to go on the pill or take any other medication, so I went to see a homeopath. It really helped to talk to someone about stuff that was bothering me at the time and she gave me some herbal remedies as well. After a while, the remedies seemed to help, and I'd begun a steady relationship, and then my periods started up again.

Now they're relatively normal again. I don't get very bad period pains, just a bit of feeling bloated because of water retention. But I've noticed that it's better and not as painful if I drink plenty of water and eat lots of fresh fruit and vegetables before my period is due – rather than pigging out on chocolate, which you often feel like doing to cheer yourself up.
(Catherine, 17)

FACT: Research has shown that girls who live together or spend a lot of time together often start and finish their periods at the same time as each other. This may be because pheromones – natural substances which smell attractive to the opposite sex – produced by one girl affect the menstrual cycles of those she's close to.

Lads and periods

It's a sad fact that lads who don't know much about periods sometimes make crass jokes about them because they feel embarrassed or awkward. But that doesn't mean that periods are anything to be ashamed or embarrassed about. Besides, no one can tell whether a girl or woman is on her period just by looking at her. And provided she washes her private parts regularly she should have no worries about iffy odours.

No-show periods

Periods can start at any time from 9 to 18 years. (If you haven't started your periods by the time you are 18 see your GP or practice nurse.) They are often irregular for the first year or so. Then they tend to settle down into a fairly regular pattern. Lots of things can interrupt this regular pattern, though, such as losing too much weight, getting very stressed or upset, becoming ill, receiving a big shock and training too hard athletically. Getting pregnant can also cause your periods to stop … but more of that later.

Breasts

aka (also known as)

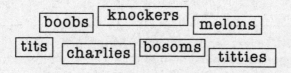

boobs knockers melons tits charlies bosoms titties

Breasts come in a vast array of different shapes and sizes. During puberty one breast sometimes grows faster than the other, but in time they do tend to even out. That said, many fully-developed women have one breast that is larger than the other all their lives, so if yours are fully-grown and still slightly lopsided, you're in good company.

Nipples also come in different shapes. Some stand out. Others are fairly flat and some look as though they've been pushed in. Pushed-in, or inverted, nipples are not a cause for concern when you're growing unless the inversion is very sudden as this may suggest breast disease.

In spite of the fact that there is no such thing as the perfect pair of breasts, some women get so het up about the size or shape of theirs, they have them enlarged or reduced surgically. Unless there is a very good reason for doing so, such drastic action is daft. The size of your bosoms will make no difference to your ability to feed a baby nor to your enjoyment of sex. What's more, most males find breasts sexy, whatever their size, and no lad worth going out with is going to be put off you because of the size of your bust.

> **FACT:** Some women have more than two breasts on their chest. The extra breasts are often little more than nipples or small bumps without nipples.

Chapter 2

sex

SEXY THOUGHTS AND RUDE URGES

All in the mind?

Puberty doesn't just affect your body. It also affects your mind. One minute your head is chock-a-block full of childhood concerns. Then next thing you know, your hormones are raging and you're experiencing all sorts of urges, fears, dreams and desires to do with romance and sex. Like the bodily changes you go through at puberty, these mind changes are just another part of growing up.

That said, sexual thoughts and urges don't hit everyone at the same time and in the same way. In fact, some people are so unexcited about sex that they are happy to let it play little or no part in their lives. If sex rarely enters your thoughts, it could be that you're not yet ready to think and feel sexually. Or maybe you are, but you just have a different level of sexual need or arousal from someone who thinks about sex a lot. Whichever way, you've got nothing to worry about.

Fruity fantasies

Daydreams and thoughts about sex are called sexual fantasies. They can pop in and out of your head in an instant or they can turn into detailed stories which last for minutes. Exploring different sexual fantasies in your head is a safe and healthy way of finding out what turns you on. Sexual fantasies can be about anything to do with sex including things that you wouldn't dream of trying in real life. There's no need to feel guilty about such fantasies. Just because they enter your head, doesn't mean that deep down you want them to happen.

Popular themes for sexual fantasies include having sex with:

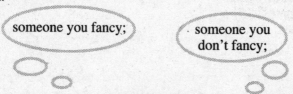

someone you fancy;

someone you don't fancy;

> members of the same sex (both gays and straights have same-sex fantasies);

> famous people.

> complete strangers;

DIY sex

Some people who enjoy fantasizing about sex do it just for the sake of it. Others like to fantasize during sex with a partner. And many enjoy fantasizing whilst they fondle, stroke or rub their own private parts. Fondling, stroking or rubbing your own private parts for pleasure is called masturbation.

> **'I sometimes imagine I'm the heroine in a historical TV series, and with one of those cool heroes when I'm masturbating. Or else I just think of one of the guys at school I really like.'**
> *(Chloe, 14)*

> **'I've got posters and magazines in my room, and I like to look at the pictures of girls I fancy. Then I let my imagination go wild while I masturbate.'**
> *(James, 15)*

40

In days gone by, masturbation was considered nothing short of evil. Many religious people thought it a terrible sin and doctors decided that it was a sure way to madness. Nowadays some people still condemn masturbation for religious reasons, but doctors and sex experts tend to agree that from a medical point of view it is perfectly harmless.

FACT: In 1908 a nurse in Britain designed and patented a cage-like contraption with spikes sticking out from it to stop boys from masturbating. This devilish device was placed over the boy's tackle and locked in place with a key.

Masturbation for males

As with all sexual activities, there are no hard and fast rules about male masturbation. However, lots of lads who masturbate do so by pulling their foreskin back and forth over the head of their penis until the penis is hard (men who are circumcised often repeatedly squeeze and release the penis instead); then they hold their erect penis firmly inside their clenched fist, and move their fist up and down smoothly in a continuous rhythm. Most lads speed up their hand movements as their excitement increases until it reaches such a peak, they ejaculate and have an orgasm (see page 43). Ejaculation and orgasm are usually the high spot of male masturbation, but some boys who can't ejaculate because they haven't started developing sperm, enjoy masturbation just for the enjoyable sensations it brings.

> **FACT:** Each male testicle produces about 2,000 sperm per second. This means that no matter how many times the testicles' owner ejaculates, he will not run out of sperm.

Masturbation for females

Girls who masturbate usually do so by touching, stroking or rubbing around and/or over the clitoris using their fingers or hand. (Because the clitoris is so sensitive, lots of girls find that they can only bear to touch theirs through the hood of skin that covers it or through the folds of flesh that surround it.) Many girls who masturbate start by gently rubbing round and round the clitoris or up and down over the clitoral area and increase the pressure and speed of their strokes as they get more turned on. If a girl is happy masturbating and keeps stimulating herself long enough, her sexual excitement will probably build to such a peak, she'll have an orgasm (see page 43).

'I find it really embarrassing talking about masturbation – somehow, it's worse even than talking about sex.'
(Hayley, 15)

To masturbate or not to masturbate ... that is the question

There are no rules about when or how often anyone should masturbate. If you don't enjoy it, or have no desire to try it, don't do it! (Just because you don't masturbate doesn't mean that you won't ever enjoy sex with a partner.) In short, unless you are so completely obsessed by masturbation that you do it all the time, everything is perfectly OK.

There is a school of thought which thinks that masturbation is shameful and only done by young boys and sad, lonely people. This is rubbish. It is quite normal for people in happy, horny sexual relationships to enjoy a spot of masturbation whenever the mood grabs them.

I've got a girlfriend, and we do a bit of heavy petting when we get the chance, and it's good. We're getting quite good about admitting what we like to do to each other, even though it was kind of awkward at first. But I still feel horny sometimes when she's not around, and I don't think there's anything wrong with having a wank in the privacy of my own bedroom.
(Jason, 16)

O is for orgasm
aka (also known as)

coming

climaxes

43

Orgasms vary from person to person and can vary from time to time in the same person. In general, however, an intense orgasm is an uncontrollable and gorgeous explosion of feeling which spreads from your private parts over your whole body. It usually wipes out all unsexy thoughts while it lasts and when it goes, it leaves you feeling blissfully relaxed.

In the build up to an orgasm both sexes usually start breathing faster and their muscles tense up. At the point of the orgasm some people let out a cry, sigh or other noise, but others make no sound at all. In other words, not everyone goes over-the-top in the grunting and groaning department when having an orgasm, despite what some feature films might lead you to believe!

Come again?

Young men usually have to wait about ten minutes or longer (sometimes much longer) after ejaculating before they can get another erection. Some girls, on the other hand, can orgasm over and over again if they continue to be stimulated. Not all girls need repeated, or multiple, orgasms to satisfy them, though. Often one good one is enough.

Chapter 3

sex

GETTING SET
FOR SEX

Virgins under pressure

FACT: In a 1994 survey of one thousand teenagers conducted by MIZZ magazine/ Brook Advisory Centres, 31 per cent of the females questioned said that they had been pressurized to lose their virginity before they were really ready.

In your teens there is a huge pressure to have sex, regardless of whether you are old enough* or mature enough to do so. Some of this pressure comes from TV, films and glossy magazines, but a lot comes from friends and classmates. Some teenagers cope with this pressure by pretending they've had sex. Then when their first time comes along, they panic because they think their partner will expect them to be an experienced lover. Others have sex simply because their friends keep on boasting that they have. Then they find out that their friends were lying and are still virgins.

'When I was in Year 10 everyone in my class said that they had "done it". By the time we all reached the sixth form everyone suddenly turned round and said they were a virgin ... everyone except me, that is. I'd really gone and "done it" in Year 10 to be like my mates.'
(Gracia , 21)

Get it right first time

Having penetrative sex for the first time (when a penis enters a vagina, mouth or anus) – is a one-off experience and not something you should rush into. It should be

*The age of consent for heterosexual (straight) couples in Britain and Northern Ireland is 16 and 17 respectively. For more information about sex and the law, turn to Chapter 9.

something you do only when you feel 100 per cent sure that you are ready. Sharing sex with someone is an extremely intimate thing to do. You expose a side of yourself that normally remains hidden and this can make you feel vulnerable and emotional. If you share your first moment of deep intimacy with someone you know really well, love, fancy and trust, and who feels the same way about you, you are likely to be in for a happy experience, even if the sex itself isn't that spectacular (and first-time sex often isn't). If you rush into things and blow your first sexual experience on someone you don't know well, who has no interest in you except as a 'shag', you may wind up feeling terrible afterwards – no matter how tough and street-wise you are.

'I think the most important thing in sex is trust. If you can't trust the other person, you can't relax with them, so you can't enjoy sex.'
(Maria, 20)

'I feel sex is something I don't want to get into yet; there's no one I know really well enough, anyway. I feel I'm too young and should wait until I feel emotionally and physically ready.'
(Katie, 15)

Sex and marriage

Some people wait until they are married before they have sex for the first time. In many cases this is because they feel that if they lose their virginity to someone to whom they are deeply committed, the whole experience will be incredibly special and loving, regardless of what the actual humpin' and pumpin' is like.

Marriage is a big step and not everyone's cup of tea, but the thinking behind saving sex for marriage is sound. Fabulous sex is not just about bodily pleasure. It's about giving and receiving love and affection. You need to be really attracted to your lover as a person, not just as a bit of crumpet, for the sex to be special. In other words, sex with someone you love and trust to bits, whether they are your partner-for-life or not, is a zillion times better than sex with someone you hardly know at all.

I definitely don't approve of sex before marriage, because I'm a Christian. It's not just on religious grounds, though. Not having sex is the best form of contraception and way of avoiding sexually transmitted diseases that there is.

I think sex should be fun. It's not just for producing children, but it's something between man and wife. Yes, I enjoy relationships, and kissing is fine; but I make it clear at the start that I don't want sex before marriage; nothing in the trouser department, please. You shouldn't touch something you haven't got. Most boys I've been out with have been friends as well, so that's OK.

I think sex is a special thing. It's like a gift you give to your husband or wife. It should be kind of celebrating the fact that you're married. If you're just boyfriend and girlfriend, and have sex, there's nothing else left to do. For some people, it's just as casual as kissing. But I think it's that full commitment that goes with marriage: like the first time of offering the whole of yourself to another person – it's as if you're new and clean and fresh – it's just very special.

So if I was going out with someone and they started coming on strong no amount of persuasion would make me agree to sex. I'd just say, 'Marry me first!'
(Anna, 16)

49

I agree with sex before marriage. Sex happens, whether you try to hide it under the carpet or not. People grow up so quickly, and you just have to deal with it. I can't see the point in marriage, if it's going to end in divorce – divorce is such a common thing now. People have kids, buy houses, sleep together without marrying – it's almost as if marriage might just disappear. I think that'd be a shame. For me, it's the ultimate commitment to someone and I only want to make that commitment once. In order to do that, you've got to be sure you're right for each other. So I think living together is a good thing.
(Maria, 20)

> **FACT:** In Emmett, Idaho, USA it is illegal for an unmarried person to have sex with another unmarried person of the opposite sex. Those who ignore the law and get caught are often sent to prison.

Check out your love

Love or lust?

Looking for true love is one thing, but knowing whether you've found it or not is another kettle of fish entirely. Many young people think they are in love one week, then realize their mistake and break up with their girl/boyfriend the next. Going out with someone you're attracted to can make your heart beat overtime, but just because you fancy the pants off each other doesn't mean that you are in love. When two people are in love, they feel a huge affection for each other. They know what makes each other tick and they feel that they can trust each other with their deepest secrets.

Fancying one another is only part of the picture. In other words, true love has as much to do with the flame in your heart as it does with the passion in your pants.

> **'I've only really had one proper girlfriend, and we've been together now for ten months. I fancied her, thought she was attractive, for about a year. Then I just woke up one morning, and knew I was in love with her. I'd rather be with her than anyone else. She always cheers me up. We've got lots of things in common: we've got the same sense of humour, and we can talk for hours about anything.'**
> *(Tom, 17)*

Crush alert

Repeatedly daydreaming about love and even marriage with a pop star, a teacher or someone else you hardly know and adore from afar is called 'having a crush'. Having a crush on someone is not the same thing as being in love with that person because broadly speaking love is something you feel for someone you have got to know well. Often your love increases as you get to know that person better. In some ways, having a major crush on someone is like a trial run for falling in love because it puts you in touch with strong romantic and sexual feelings.

It must be love!

Being in love and being desperate to be in love are also easily confused. Some people convince themselves that they are in love with practically everyone they go out with because they want to be in a loving relationship. Wanting to be in love is no crime but it often pays to look at any relationship you have carefully and think about how well you and your boy/girlfriend really know each other before you announce your love. That way you can examine your own feelings more clearly, and avoid hurting your boy/ girlfriend by letting them think you love them when you don't.

Put your love to the test

Falling in love and being in love with someone who you suspect may not be in love with you can be heartbreaking. One way of finding out how an unromantic boy/girlfriend truly feels is to tell them that you love them in a non-sexual situation and see how they react. If your boy/ girlfriend feels uncomfortable with what you say, you need to know why.

FACT: It is said that phenylethylamine, a chemical produced by the brain, is responsible for the wonderful highs you feel when you are in love or sexually attracted to someone. This same chemical can be found in chocolate.

Hot to trot? Ready or not?

My first remotely sexual experience was when I was about 14. I had no idea what I was doing; it just happened. It was in her bedroom: we were close together, and somehow she guided my hand inside her shirt ... and it was the most natural thing in the world for me to slip my hand inside her bra. I had never before seen, let alone touched, a girl's breasts. My excitement was intense – in fact, later she said that I was shaking as I moved. There's no other feeling like that sexual excitement – kind of breathless.

I remember sort of feeling I'd got an advantage over my friends, but at the same time I felt even more in love with my girlfriend. I also realized how easily we could get carried away. But as our relationship carried on, we got more and more serious about the types of things we did, such as moving to parts of the anatomy below the waist.

I think I'm the type of person who ... well, although I do enjoy the sexual aspect of a relationship, I also need to love the person I am with. So, when I found that my love for the girl I was with was dwindling, I began to feel a bit guilty. I knew that, if I did carry on as though nothing was wrong, we could easily lose our virginity together. I think now that, as a 14-year-old, my sexual urges were more intense – certainly the idea of losing my virginity before my 15th birthday was very inviting. But I still had the feeling that I couldn't carry on doing 'naughty things' with someone I didn't love. It wouldn't be fair on either of us.
(Bob, 16)

OK. So you think you've found someone special, and you want to make your relationship a sexual one ... but are you really ready for sex? Ask yourself these questions:

1. Are my girl/boyfriend and I old enough to have sex legally? Y N

2. Am I sure that he/she is the right person for me and that we have chosen the right time and place to have sex? Y N

3. Do we trust each other enough to be able to talk openly together about our feelings? Y N

4. Do I think that I will be able to cope with the feelings of vulnerability, closeness or possessiveness that either of us may feel after sex? Y N

5. If my boy/girlfriend gets really turned on and I then change my mind about going any further, would I have the courage to say 'stop!'? Y N

6. If my boy/girlfriend gets me turned on and then doesn't want to go any further, would I respect their wishes and stop? Y N

7. Have we discussed safer sex and birth control and both agreed to use a condom? Y N

8. Has my desire to have sex got a lot to do with the fact that all my friends say that they've 'done it'? Y N

9. Do I want to have sex to impress my mates because they fancy my boy/girlfriend too? Y N

10. Do I mainly want to have sex because I'm afraid that my girl/boyfriend will dump me if I don't? Y N

11. Have I been putting pressure on my boy/girlfriend to go further than they really want to?	Ⓨ Ⓝ
12. Do I mainly want to have sex to please my girl/boyfriend because we've been going out for a long time and they have been patient about our not having sex?	Ⓨ Ⓝ
13. Will having sex at this time lead to either of us getting hurt?	Ⓨ Ⓝ

If you answered YES to questions 1-7, and NO to questions 8-13, you may very well be ready to have sex. But before you start a-movin' and a-groovin', read Chapters 6 and 7 to make sure that you know exactly how to use a condom to protect yourself and your partner from sexually transmitted infections and how to choose, or help your partner choose, some form of back-up contraception to protect against unwanted pregnancy.

If you answered NO to any of the first seven questions or YES to any of the last six, you need to stop in your tracks, put your passion on hold and read the rest of this chapter carefully.

Sex and the law

It is against the law to have sex if you are under the age of consent. (If you aren't sure whether you are old enough to have sex legally, turn to Chapter 9 to find out.) However, just because you are over the age of consent, it doesn't automatically mean that you are ready to start a sexual relationship. So, don't feel pressurized to have sex just because you're in your late teens.

Sex with a stranger

Having sex with someone who you don't know very well can be dangerous. For all you know they could be the sort of immature idiot who goes around telling everyone what you are like in bed. Or, worse still, they could be the sort of person who will try and force you to do things you don't want to do and not take 'stop!' for an answer.

And that's not all. Having sex can open up a floodgate of feelings which means that even if you and your 'stranger' start off having sex for sex's sake, without any thought of developing a relationship, you may find yourself feeling more emotional towards them after sex because you feel vulnerable. Coping with rejection, if your 'stranger' turns out to feel differently, can be really tough.

Sex and the green-eyed monster

Changing a relationship into a sexual one is often a mighty big step and it can leave you feeling much more possessive about your boy/girlfriend and them about you. If you think that either of you would prefer to keep things casual, you might be better off waiting until you both feel the same way.

Remember, you don't have to have sex with everyone you go out with, even if you've had sex before. Nor do you have to 'go the whole way' with your partner to have fun. Kissing, hugging and caressing can be just as pleasurable as having penetrative sex.

Saying no

Saying NO in a sexual situation isn't always easy, but that's no excuse for having sex when you really don't want to. Just because you've flirted with someone doesn't mean that you have to get sexual with them. Kissing, fondling or 'going all the way' when you're not in the mood can be damaging as it can leave you hating your partner, sex and yourself.

If you feel that your boy/girlfriend is going further than you want to sexually, let them know clearly and directly.

Use your body language to back up what you're saying. Don't think 'I'm not sure about this, but I'll see how it goes before I say anything.' Take control of the situation the minute you're in doubt and say something like 'Whoa! This is all going a little too fast for me. Can we just take things a bit slower?' If you don't want to do anything frisky, and yet don't want to hurt your boy/girlfriend's feelings, try explaining kindly and gently why you don't feel in the mood and suggest perhaps a cuddle or a chat instead. That way you should be able to minimize your own embarrassment and help stop your partner from feeling hurt or rejected.

'...but if you loved me you would'

No one should ever be forced into having sex to prove that they love someone. If you're not ready to have sex and your boy/girlfriend says '...but if you loved me you'd have sex with me', simply tell them that if they loved you, they'd respect your wish to wait. If your boy/girlfriend decides that they can't wait, and as a result dumps you, you'll probably feel badly hurt. But you won't feel anywhere near as badly hurt as you would have done had you had sex for the wrong reasons.

And another thing. Remember – penetrative sex is not the be-all and end-all of a loving relationship. Hugging, kissing and stroking can be just as enjoyable as full-blown sex; they are also wonderful ways of showing someone that you care for them.

Putting pressure on a partner

No one has a right to sex, no matter how horny they're feeling. If you are guilty of putting pressure on someone to go further than they want to sexually, you may well be on the way to ruining what was or might have been a great relationship. Besides, if that person does give in to your pressure and has sex with you grudgingly, it is highly likely that they will find the whole experience disappointing or hateful – which won't say much for your status as a stud or saucepot.

'You're frigid!'

One way of putting pressure on someone who won't go as far sexually as you would like is to accuse them of being cold or 'frigid'. This implies that the person under pressure is unable to have sexual feelings. If you've ever accused a partner of being 'frigid', take note. Everyone is capable of enjoying sex with the right person, in the right place and at the right time. In other words, your partner's 'frigidity' probably had less to do with their hatred of sex and more to do with the fact that they just weren't ready to have sex with you.

Blue balls!

Some lads try to pressurize their girlfriends into having sex by saying that if a man gets really turned on and doesn't have an orgasm, he'll be racked with pain – a condition known as 'blue balls'. This is a load of old tosh! When a man has an orgasm, all the blood that has rushed into his penis and given him an erection rushes out again. If he gets sexually excited but doesn't have an orgasm, the blood in his erect penis simply drains away more slowly. Until this happens he may feel uncomfortable in the ball department but he's not in any danger. Similarly, girls who get very turned on and then don't have an orgasm may find that their private parts ache for a bit, but this doesn't do them any harm physically.

Safer sex

Penetrative sex without contraception equals risky sex. It's as simple as that! If you think using contraception is too embarrassing, too much effort or too unromantic READ CHAPTERS 6 AND 7. Unless you are unbelievably stupid, the information there will make you change your mind.

Talking about sex

Coping with the ups and downs of a close relationship, and thinking about or deciding to have sex for the first time can leave you feeling anxious. Talking to someone you trust about your feelings can help. Parents are often the ideal adults to talk to, but you may feel too embarrassed to talk to your own parents about something as saucy as sex. Admittedly, sexuality is not an easy topic of conversation for many parents because they find it hard to accept that their children have now become sexual beings. (That said, many young adults find the idea that their parents have ever had sex, let alone still do have sex, more than a little unnerving!) But that doesn't mean to say that your parents can't listen carefully and be helpful and understanding.

If you feel you can't talk to your parents or guardians, you could talk to another responsible adult you really trust and who cares about you or you could contact one of the young people's organizations at the back of this book, such as a Brook Advisory Centre. Staff at Brook can help you decide if you are ready to have sex.

Chatting to your friends about sex is fine too, especially if you all share genuine feelings and fears, but make sure you double-check any advice or tips you are given. Just because a friend has bonked their way to Timbuktu and back doesn't mean they know everything there is to know about sex.

Chapter 4

sex

SEX: THE INS AND OUTS

Use your imagination

Having sex is a natural part of adulthood, but just because someone is old enough and mature enough emotionally to have a sexual relationship doesn't mean that they automatically know how to be a sex sensation! (For information about the all-important emotional side of sex, see Chapter 3.) It takes time to be a good lover. You need to learn what pleases you and what pleases your partner. You need to feel relaxed, happy and safe with each other. And you need to use your imagination.

Losing my virginity didn't really live up to my expectations. My mum and dad had gone away on holiday, and we were in my room ... I just felt guilty; I knew they wouldn't be happy about it happening. I was physically ready for it, quite mature, and lots of my friends had had sex already. Dave pushed me from the word go; I had to fend him off, really: and I did make him wait till I'd been on the pill for a couple of weeks.

We progressed naturally, I suppose, from snogging and touching to sex. The earth didn't move for me, though – and I felt as though he didn't make any effort to make sure it did. He never asked if I was ready. It was very one-sided, really. I was also terrified the first time: of the intimacy; letting him in, mentally, not just physically. He'd know so much about me. You're at your most vulnerable once sex is involved. I wasn't sure if I could trust him not to run and tell his mates every detail – whether he was genuine, that he really cared.
(Lizzie, 17)

Sex isn't just about penetration. It is also about lip kissing, neck nuzzling, thigh stroking, toe sucking, skin tickling, body rubbing, ear nibbling, bosom fondling, bottom squeezing, blowing down the back of a neck ... and a whole host of other delicious activities besides.

The great thing about these sexy activities is that they don't usually involve blood or sexual fluids, such as vaginal juices and semen, passing from one person's body into another's. This means that they don't carry the same risks as penetrative sex with regard to starting a pregnancy or catching HIV, the virus that can lead to AIDS. HOWEVER, before you decide to try and do anything remotely saucy with your partner, you must read Chapters 6 and 7. Chapter 7 tells you how you can reduce the risk of catching HIV and other sexually transmitted infections. And Chapter 6 explains how pregnancy happens. Once you know how HIV and pregnancy occur, you and your partner will be able to work out which sexual activities you can enjoy safely without using protection.

French kissing

aka (also known as)

snogging   having a tongue sarnie

deep kissing

There is no right way to French kiss, but the basics involve one person pressing their slightly-open and relaxed lips against another person's slightly-open and relaxed lips and then exploring each other's mouths with their tongues. Described in black and white, it doesn't sound too tasty, but when done with the right person at the right time and in the right place, French kissing can be a truly blissful pastime.

If you're new to French kissing, or you've tried it and didn't rate it, here are a few tips you may find handy.

It often pays off to approach your partner's mouth carefully, with your lips slightly parted. No one likes being whacked in the mouth by an over-forceful kisser. Nor do they want to have a good look at your dental work as you head towards them.

One way to French kiss (and there are many) is to start by gently touching your partner's lips with your own and then pressing your lips more firmly to theirs, while at the same time opening and closing your mouth very slightly and gently exploring the front of your partner's tongue with your own. If you keep your tongue relaxed, don't press your lips too hard or open your mouth too wide, you should be fine.

The best French kisses are those that involve both partners doing whatever comes naturally. However, as most kissers would agree, dribbling and stiff tongues are definite no-nos, as is churning your tongue round and round as though it were a helicopter propeller preparing for take-off.

It's a good idea to be aware of how your partner is responding to your kisses. That way you'll know whether to step up the passion, ease it off slightly or call it a day and go home!

Finally, no one likes kissing a foul-smelling mouth, but if you brush your teeth regularly and avoid smoking and eating strong-smelling foods before you start kissing, you should have no problems.

'Kissing for ages makes me feel kind of high
– and like going on!'
(Scott, 18)

FACT: It is rumoured that each kiss you have takes
one to three minutes off your life. This is a load of
baloney.

'When I was about 12, I went out with a girl.
What she didn't realize was that I had got a
brace. We were kissing, and suddenly I
realized that her chewing gum had got
caught in my brace. It took ages getting it
out – I had to use a toothpick.'
(Carl, 16)

'When I first kissed someone – well, he
kissed me first – I thought it was horrible, all
wet and slobbery. It's better now, though,
now I'm older; I know different ways of
doing it.'
(Katie, 15)

Exploring erogenous zones

Having a really good snog together is just one way in which two people can please each other sexually without 'going all the way'. Massaging each other with scented oils is an equally sexy and satisfying thing to do. So is stroking a partner's body or hair, gently scratching them from neck to toe, blowing down their neck, whispering romantic things into their ear, dancing with them in the nude etc.

The areas of the body that make a person feel sexually aroused when they are touched, stroked, licked, sucked or kissed are called erogenous zones. Genitals and breasts are usually pretty high up on most people's list of erogenous zones, but ears, neck, arms, fingers, legs, stomach, back and toes are often not very far behind. Different areas excite different people, so it pays if both partners are sensitive to each other's preferences.

'I really like it when my girlfriend sucks my fingers.'
(Iain, 21)

'Stroking my hair: that's lovely, it feels so good.'
(Deborah, 19)

'You can't get much more sensual than being given a massage.'
(Ben, 21)

Mutual masturbation

Mutual masturbation usually involves each partner masturbating the other to give them pleasure. However, that said, mutual masturbation can also include one partner masturbating in front of the other, to get them both sexually excited. (See pages 42-44 for more details about male and female masturbation.)

Masturbating someone is a big step up from kissing them or nibbling their ear, so it's important that both partners are well and truly ready to get very intimate with each other before they try their hands at mutual masturbation. (See Chapter 3 for more information on getting set for sex).

On a practical level it's also important that both partners take care that no semen ends up in or near the girl's vaginal opening. Sperm can swim from the vaginal lips up into the vagina causing either a pregnancy or the spread of infection.

Semen or vaginal fluids which end up in cuts and grazes on fingers or other parts of the body may also lead to infection, so it makes sense for both partners to ensure that their hands are clean, their fingernails are smooth and any sores or cuts are well covered before they masturbate each other. (See Chapters 6 and 7 for more information on how to avoid pregnancy and sexually transmitted infections.)

FACT: Sprurting semen doesn't usually travel that far, but it can cover a distance of up to 60 cm ... and if it lands in an eye, it can sting!

Oral sex
aka (also known as)

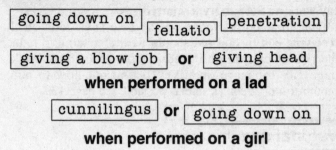

going down on   fellatio   penetration

giving a blow job **or** giving head

when performed on a lad

cunnilingus **or** going down on

when performed on a girl

Oral sex involves kissing, licking and sucking someone else's private parts, or genitals. As with all sexual acts, there are no hard and fast rules about how oral sex should be performed. However, in general, mouth-to-penis sex involves the girl wrapping her lips around her partner's erect penis, sucking in slightly and moving her mouth up and down, so that his penis slides in and out between her lips at a steady rhythm: and, generally speaking, mouth-to-vulva sex involves the lad gently kissing, licking and sucking his partner's clitoris and the area around it. Neither of these kinds of sex has to lead to orgasm or ejaculation, but if the person doing the deed keeps on going, chances are they will.

Oral sex is an extremely intimate type of sex – can you think of anything more intimate than burying your face in someone else's nether regions? – and while some people adore it, others regard it as little short of a criminal act! Those who are worried about trying oral sex often fear that they will smell or taste awful to their partner or vice versa, but the truth is vaginal juices and semen only smell or taste awful if they are infected and private parts only tend to smell iffy when they are not washed regularly. In fact, the natural smell of a clean vulva or scrotum can be rather gorgeous. That said, like all the other sexual activities described in this chapter, oral sex is not a compulsory part of a sexual relationship. So, if the very thought of the deed makes your stomach churn, don't worry. There's no rule to say you ever have to try it yourself.

One final point: to be on the safe side, lads on the receiving end of oral sex should wear a condom to reduce the risk of passing on infection through their semen (see page 139 for more details). To find out how to make mouth-to-vulva-sex as safe as possible see page 139.

Vaginal sex

aka (also known as)

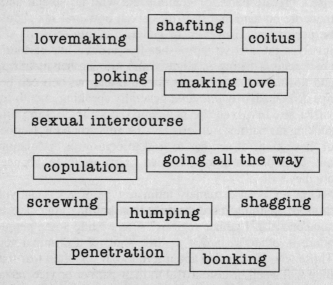

lovemaking · shafting · coitus · poking · making love · sexual intercourse · copulation · going all the way · screwing · humping · shagging · penetration · bonking

Having vaginal sex with someone is a very intimate thing to do. Mechanically speaking, this type of sex involves an erect penis sliding up and down inside a vagina. The owner of the penis can either slide his penis into the vagina himself, or his partner can help guide it in using her hand or by moving her body into a helpful position.

'I wouldn't expect to go all the way straight away: it would be a fair while into the relationship. It depends how well you get on; you need to be really good friends.'
(Carl, 16)

Foreplay

On the whole, couples tend to lead up to vaginal sex by doing some or all of the activities already described, such as kissing, hugging, caressing, fondling and masturbating each other. When these saucy activities are done as a lead up to vaginal sex they are called foreplay.

'Licking my ear, or nibbling it – even when he just breathes into it – really turns me on.'
(Kirsty, 18)

'Being tickled really gets me going.'
(Terry, 22)

'I love it when she strokes the inside of my thighs.'
(Liam, 20)

71

'Being stroked all over is really sexy.'
(Hayley, 20)

Indulging in some sort of foreplay before vaginal intercourse begins is usually a good idea because it helps to relax and excite both lovers, and vaginal sex is easier and more enjoyable if both lovers are really turned-on before it begins. This is particularly true for girls who, if not fully relaxed, may tense up the muscles in their vaginas which can make penetration by a penis painful. Getting turned-on before penetration begins is also useful because the excitement gets a girl's vaginal juices flowing and the 'wetter' her vagina is, the more comfortable she'll feel when her lover's penis is moving inside her.

One other thing worth knowing about vaginal sex is this. Male thrusting doesn't usually last that long – a few minutes is not unusual – and once a lad has ejaculated, his interest in sex quickly dwindles, for a while at least. So if a girl doesn't have time to get excited before vaginal sex begins, she could end up feeling disappointed when the deed is done.

The positions

There are lots of different positions in which couples can have vaginal sex. These positions include the woman lying down with her legs apart and the man lying on top of her; the man lying down with his knees slightly bent and the woman sitting straddled over him; and the woman kneeling down on all fours with the man entering her vagina from behind.

Lads usually find it easy to 'come' during vaginal sex, but many girls don't. That's not to say that girls don't enjoy the feeling of a penis inside them. It's just that many girls need to have their clitoris stimulated during penetration to make the whole experience more physically satisfying. Good positions clitoris-wise are those which leave a pair of hands free to touch the clitoris and anything else besides. Man-on-top positions can be good clitoris-wise too, if the lad's body presses down on the clitoral area and moves it about.

The G-spot
aka (also known as)

```
the sacred spot
```

Sexual positions, such as rear-entry ones, in which the penis presses upward against the front inside wall of the vagina are good for stimulating a girl's G-spot. The G-spot – which is named after Dr Graftenberg, the gynaecologist who is credited with discovering it – is an erogenous zone on the front inside wall of the vagina about halfway between the opening and the cervix. Many women couldn't tell you where their G-spot is if you paid them, so clearly a girl doesn't have to know where her G-spot is to enjoy sex. (In fact, some people reckon that the G-spot doesn't even exist.) However, a number of women who believe that it does say that if this super sensitive area is massaged by a penis or a finger it can lead to an orgasm … and this orgasm can be accompanied by a gush of liquid from the urethra which isn't pee. So, if you're a female and one day you find yourself fast approaching a G-spot orgasm, forget about wetting yourself – and go with the flow.

Anal sex

aka (also known as)

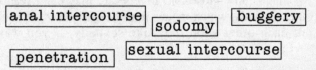

```
anal intercourse    sodomy    buggery

penetration    sexual intercourse
```

Put most simply, anal sex involves a man thrusting his erect penis in and out of someone else's anus until he ejaculates. Anal sex isn't a common sexual activity between hetero-sexual couples. Nor is it an essential part of gay male sex, so no one should ever feel that this type of sex is something they should be doing. Unlike the vagina, the back passage, or rectum, isn't designed for sex and so isn't naturally wet or stretchy which means that anal sex can hurt.

Anal sex is very dodgy infections-wise because the back passage tears easily when penetrated and, because it is tight, it puts a lot of strain on a condom. To make things safer, the person penetrating should always wear an ultra strong/extra thick condom and smear water-based lubricant on the outside of it (for more details about condoms and lubrication see Chapter 6). He should also always enter his partner's anus slowly and gently, and be prepared to stop when asked.

Talking of infections, it is worth knowing that any penis, finger etc. that has been up a bottom must always be given a fresh condom or washed carefully before it goes anywhere near a vagina or mouth. Germs from a bottom which are passed on to a vagina or mouth can cause horrid infections.

> **FACT:** Up until 1994, anal sex between heterosexual or straight adults was illegal in England and Wales. Nowadays, anal sex is only legal if both partners are willing and aged 18 or over.

Sex talk

No matter how close two lovers are, they can't read each other's minds, which means that they may have to show or tell each other what they like sexually. If you want to

74

change something that your partner is doing to you, you can either take their hand and guide their movements or you can give them some verbal guidance. 'Slower', 'faster', 'harder', 'softer' are often the only words you need. If you want to be more specific, make sure you're not critical. The way to ask for change is to stress what you like rather than harp on about what you don't like. In other words saying 'I love it when you hold my penis firmly' will go down a lot better than saying 'Have you lost the strength in your right hand or what?' Similarly, saying 'I'd really love it if you would…' will get better results than saying 'Stop that, you pervert! It hurts!'

Lost motorists are not the only ones who need directions, so if you're not sure whether your partner is enjoying something that you are doing to them, ask. Looking into their eyes and listening to the sounds they make will give you some clues, but asking directly will make things clearer if you're really not sure. Say something like 'Does that feel good?' or 'Am I touching you right?' Provided you stop short of full-scale interrogation, you should get the information you want without making your partner feel under the spotlight.

Incidentally, saying when something feels extra good and making appreciative noises are generous things to do because the more you let your partner know how fabulous they make you feel, the happier they'll be.

Picking up sex clues

It is a smart idea to pay attention to what your lover does to you when you are playing together because, without realizing it, they may be doing to you exactly what they would like you to do to them. In other words, if your partner spends a long time nibbling your ear or squeezing your bottom, chances are that they would love you to return the favour.

Close of play

One of the loveliest things about sex is the snuggling up afterwards. This part isn't essential – and if your steamy sex session has made you late for crochet class, it may not be possible – but if you and your partner can find the time to cuddle up close for a bit, you're unlikely to regret it. Having sex can be a pretty intense experience and if you both leap up afterwards and hurry on your way, you may feel slightly disorientated.

False starts, fumbles and fears

Sexy films and lovey-dovey books are fine if you want entertainment, but they are no good if you want to learn about real-life sex. In films you often see two virtual strangers bonking their way to the heights of ecstasy without so much as the hint of a wilting willy. In real life sex is not always that easy.

Below you'll find some of the most common sexual problems and their solutions. It's worth reading this section in full as lads' problems affect girls and vice versa. Most sexual problems can be solved if both partners are honest about their needs and want each other to be happy and satisfied. That said, sexual problems sometimes have a physical cause which needs medical treatment. If you keep having sexual problems and find that the tips here don't help, it might be worth seeing a doctor. If your problem turns out to be a psychological one, getting referred to a trained counsellor may do wonders.

Males

First-time nerves

Even couples who love, fancy and trust each other, some-times suffer from a flutter of nerves the first time they have sex. If you and your partner are emotionally ready for sex, but still feel a little nervous, make sure you choose somewhere private and comfortable where you can have sex undisturbed. Not rushing things will help too, particularly if your partner is also a virgin. The **Females** section over the page gives some useful tips about when to start penetration and which position you might like to start with. Lads new to sex often find it helps to enter their partner's vagina gently but firmly and to start by thrusting lightly. If your partner is a virgin, make sure you don't thrust too deeply at first.

'Coming' too quickly

'Coming' too quickly (i.e. ejaculating before or very soon after starting penetrative sex) is such a common problem amongst young men that you'd be hard pushed to find a lad to whom it has never happened. Like most common sexual 'problems', the secret is *not* to worry that it is going to happen each time you have sex. Otherwise the very fact that you're worrying could make it happen.

One practical solution to the problem of 'coming' too quickly, or premature ejaculation, is to masturbate before you have sex, or let your partner do this for you. The idea is that if you've 'come' once, it will take the edge off your excitement and so you will probably be able to last longer before you 'come' again. Even if you are not having sex with your partner but find that you 'come' really quickly when the two of you are having a kiss and a cuddle, a quick hand-job before you both meet up may help stop you getting overexcited too quickly.

Another way of coping with 'coming' very quickly during penetrative sex is to forget about it, relax, concentrate on your partner's pleasure and then, when your penis is stiff again, try again.

Some lads find it helps to move their hips in a circle when they enter their partner's vagina rather than thrusting them back and forth. (Circular hip movements tend to move the penis in a less stimulating way than thrusting ones.) Others find that women-on-top positions slow things down as the penis is not stimulated so vigorously in this position as in others.

Unless your partner is horribly uncaring, she shouldn't have any problems with you 'coming' too quickly provided that you give her lots of love and affection and make sure that she is satisfied sexually.

Losing an erection

Lots of young men find it hard to get or keep an erection at some time or other. Feeling nervous, tired, depressed or under pressure to be 'good' in bed can make the stiffest of willies wilt. So too can not really feeling in the mood, not being ready emotionally to 'go all the way' or being worried.

If you are sure that you are emotionally ready for a sexual relationship, but have trouble keeping an erection because you're trying too hard to please, don't worry. Instead try and make sure that you only have sex when you are really in the mood; and take time to enjoy your partner's body without worrying about what your willy is doing. If it goes limp at a crucial moment, stay calm, explain to your partner that you are too tired or unready for penetration, and ask if you can enjoy just kissing, cuddling and fondling each other instead. Once you and your partner discover that you can enjoy yourselves sexually without 'going the whole way', you will probably be less worried about losing your erection next time round.

If you want to try and do something about overcoming this problem whilst on your own you might find it helpful to try the following technique. Find somewhere private and masturbate until you have a full erection. Stop what you are doing, think some unsexy thoughts, and let your erection go down. Do this once more, then masturbate again and this time carry on until you 'come'. Keep doing this exercise until you feel confident that you can regain an erection after you've lost it. This confidence should help you when you come to have sex with your partner.

> **FACT:** In sixteenth to eighteenth-century France, not being able to get and use an erection were almost the only grounds on which the Church would grant a divorce. So public trials were set up in which husbands had to prove to the world that their private parts were in good working order.

Females

First-time nerves

Many girls fear that first-time sex will hurt because their boyfriend's penis will be too big for them. Erect willies can look eye-wateringly large, it's true, but the vagina is elastic and can stretch to fit around whatever it contains, including a baby.

If you are very nervous about making love for the first time and have never used a tampon, you could try stretching your vaginal opening a little with clean fingers. Start by covering your middle finger with lots of lubricant (see page 113). Gently push it up into your vagina bit by bit and at the same time strain slightly as though you were pushing something out of your vagina. This will stop the vagina from tightening up. Stop whenever you begin to feel uptight and take a few deep breaths. If/when you've managed to push your whole finger in, start again using two fingers. By doing this you should be able to get rid of any nervousness you may feel about penetration.

Big willies are not the only things which make some girls nervous about first-time sex. There are a number of stories around which make out that losing your virginity has to be painful and bloody because it involves the breaking of the hymen. Now, as you know if you've read page 25, many girls have very little hymen left by the time they are young women and so experience little if any pain or bleeding when they first have sex. It is only if your hymen is especially tough and intact that first-time sex may be more painful. If you've got a tough hymen and you want to stretch it before you start having sex, try pushing on it gently with a clean finger.

Another way to help overcome first-time nerves is to tell your partner that you are a virgin and ask him to go gently at first. There is nothing uncool about being a virgin. *Everyone is a virgin at some stage in their lives* and most lads, like most girls, would be delighted to know that they were the first person to make love with their partner. If any lad or girl finds their partner's virginity a joke or something to sneer at, the problem is theirs, not their partner's.

For more tips about making first-time sex easier read 'First-time nerves' in the **Males'** section (see page 76) and 'Pain during penetration' below.

Pain during penetration

If you've already had vaginal sex a few times and found it painful, chances are your vagina wasn't producing enough natural juices. This could be a sign that you are not yet ready emotionally for sex. Or maybe you are, but are just rushing things. If you think you fall into the latter category, take things more slowly the next time you make love and make sure you are really relaxed and turned-on before you let your boyfriend's penis inside you. Remember, the more relaxed and turned-on you are before penetration begins, the wetter your vagina will be and the easier it will be for the penis to slide in and out.

If you want extra help on the wetness front, you could use a lubricated condom (see page 110) or smear some lubrication on the outside of the condom (see page 113) before penetration begins. This will make penetration easier and lessen your chances of feeling sore afterwards. You could also strain slightly, as though you were pushing something out of your vagina, as your boyfriend's penis enters you. This will stop your vagina from tightening up. Many couples new to sex find that getting the penis inside the vagina is easiest if the girl has her knees bent and her thighs wide apart, and if she or her partner gently holds her vaginal lips open with one hand while she helps her partner guide his penis into her vagina.

Vaginal shutdown

Some girls get so tense at the thought of penetration by a penis that their vaginal muscles clamp shut at the first hint of sex. Sometimes this is a signal that the girl isn't ready emotionally to have sex with her partner. Occasionally there is a physical reason for this condition which can be sorted out by a doctor. If neither of these cases apply, learning to relax and getting really turned-on before penetration begins usually helps a lot. Some girls who suffer from this condition find it helps to insert a finger or two inside their vagina as described in 'First-time nerves', to help get rid of their fear about vaginal penetration. Others find it easier to be on top during sex because that way they have more control over how slowly and gently their boyfriend's penis enters them. If you find you suffer from vaginal shutdown you might find that the best thing to do is to forget penetration for the time being, have a kiss and cuddle and whatever else feels comfortable, and try again another time. Remember, it's perfectly OK for you to stop sex at any time, if you feel anxious or unhappy.

Desperately seeking orgasms

There is so much nonsense talked about orgasms these days that it may come as a surprise to you to learn that you don't have to have an orgasm to have a good time sexually. However if you want to experience one with your partner and you've had no luck so far, you might find it useful to try a little DIY sex! To start with, find somewhere private and comfortable and touch and stroke your body all over to discover what feels good. Take your time and don't be shy. By doing all this, you'll soon discover what lights you up, which means you'll be able to show your partner the kind of stimulation you need to get you going.

Whatever you do, don't get into the habit of faking orgasms because you want to please your partner or get sex over and done with as quickly as possible. Faking orgasms can lead your partner to think you're having a great time when you're not, and this can store up problems for the future. What's more, if your partner discovers you've faked it even just once, it could destroy their trust in you. So, if you want to have real orgasms with your partner, you have to be honest and try out different things together to see what works best for you.

High hopes and unreal expectations

If you have unreal expectations about sex i.e. you think that the earth will move and the stars shake every time you do it, you are setting yourself up for a big disappointment. Even the most experienced lovers find that while sex is great some of the time, it is often just pleasantly OK. First-time sex in particular is rarely the stuff of saucy films or racy novels. That's not to say that losing your virginity can't be a lovely, bonding experience. It's just that sex tends to improve with practice.

'The girlfriend I'm with at the moment, we get on really well, we're really close friends too. We're kind of both learning together, we don't know it all straight away: it all becomes clearer the more you have sex together.'
(Carl, 16)

> **FACT**: According to sex counsellors, some married couples who are religious don't have sex. This is because the first time these couples tried it, it seemed so disappointing compared with the heavenly, holy experience that they had been expecting, they never finished it or tried it again.

Having realistic expectations about sex also makes it easier to shrug off the deeply unsexy things that can happen during sex, such as burps, hiccups and the farting sound a vagina sometimes makes when a penis is pulled out of it. If you accept that natural noises such as these and other unromantic things can happen during sex, and you're prepared to ignore them or share a giggle about them, they won't spoil your fun.

One last point about unreal expectations. Many people who hate their own bodies find it hard to believe that anyone will find them sexy. But what these people don't realize is that bodily perfection does not automatically equal sex appeal. The secret of sex appeal is confidence. If you like yourself and are confident about yourself in general, this will spill over into your love life. And if you are secure in your sex appeal, chances are that any lover you have will be happy to accept you as you are, lardy thighs and all.

Talking of lardy thighs, tubby torsos, Concorde noses and the like, people who moan on and on about how unattractive they look tend to leave others cold. So if you want to get your partner nicely in the mood, it's best not to start by giving them a critical tour of your weird or wobbly bits.

'I think personality matters more in a girl than looks: if she's funny, easy to talk to, if you feel you can be friends. I suppose that's what "going out" is at first: it's when you can be a special friend for each other.'
(Carl, 16)

Chapter 5

sex

GLAD TO
BE GAY

A lot of people grow up to be heterosexual, or straight. That means they mainly fancy people of the opposite sex. Those who don't grow up in this way are either homosexual, i.e. gay or lesbian – that means that they mainly fancy people of the same sex as themselves – or else they are bisexual, or bi, which means that they are strongly attracted to both sexes.

I first knew I was gay when I was quite young, about 10. I didn't know what gay meant – I just felt I was different from the other boys: they'd talk about girls and I didn't get it. All the way through secondary school, I didn't know who I was, why I felt the way I did. I sort of had girlfriends, but it didn't amount to much. Once I had sex with a girl – it was on holiday, and it was fine – but after a while we didn't keep in touch. I finally came out when I was on the streets, at Pride [a gay festival], *last year.*
(Josh, 18)

I've always known, in a way, that I'm bisexual – but I kind of put off the thought because I had so many other problems: parents splitting up and so on. I was really confused because I fancied women and I also fancied men. I thought, 'Well, I'll just have to tell people I'm a lesbian who enjoys sex with men.' Then I had to fill in a form for college and it said, 'Bisexual' – and I thought, 'Wow, I really exist!'
(Keely, 17)

Gay sex

Heterosexual people sometimes wonder what homosexual couples get up to in bed. And the answer is, much the same thing as straight couples. In other words kissing, cuddling, fondling, stroking, mutual masturbation, oral sex and snuggling up afterwards are just as much a part of gay sex as they are of straight sex. (For more nitty gritty information about these and other sexual activities see Chapter 4. For information about the laws concerning gay sex see page 167.)

There is a belief amongst some straight people that sex between gay men always includes anal sex, but this is not the case. True, many gay men do enjoy having anal sex, but it is not a compulsory part of lad-with-lad sex and not all gay couples do it.

'Personally I'm not a big fan of anal sex – a lot of people think that's the only thing to do if you're gay – but I think oral sex is much more satisfying. I suppose it's a matter of individual taste.'
(Josh, 18)

There are also some misinformed people who think that lesbian sex is just about one girl strapping on a fake willy, or dildo, and pretending to be a man. Admittedly there are some lesbian couples who enjoy using a fake willy as part of their love play, but this kind of fun is hardly the be-all-and-end-all of lesbian sex. Firstly, as you'll know if you've read Chapter 4, girls don't need to be penetrated by a penis to achieve orgasm; and secondly, lesbians are turned-on by girls' bodies, not lads' bodies – that's the whole point – so it stands to reason that a willy is not an essential ingredient of lesbian sex.

I realized I liked women when I was 18, and kissed my best friend. Women somehow have more natural empathy. In my experience, sex with women is satisfying in a different way from with men. There's more foreplay, for one thing. If you're hungry, you can go out and grab some fish and chips and wolf it down; and it's satisfying in a way – that's sex with a man. Or you can go out for a really fancy meal, with lots of courses, trying out some new and exotic dishes, plenty of variety, and have really good wine with it, get gently pissed, and it's really nice – that's sex with a woman.
(Anne, 23)

Am I gay?

Sexuality can be a changing thing. Some teenagers develop crushes on people of the same sex and then go on to have happy heterosexual relationships. Others start out dating people of the opposite sex and later on in life fall for someone of their own sex. And many know from an early age that they are either straight or gay and never change their minds about this.

If you are not sure where you stand – perhaps because you fantasize about one sex and yet enjoy dating the other, or because you are mainly attracted to the opposite sex and yet have the serious hots for someone of your own sex – don't worry. Young adults often feel unsure about their sexuality and some find that they need to try a variety of relationships with both sexes before they discover what their sexual identity is. If you are really troubled with uncertainty you could talk to someone you know and trust who is gay and/or you could ring your local gay and lesbian switchboard or the London Lesbian and Gay Switchboard which aims to provide advice, information and counselling for the whole of the UK. See page 186 for details.

Gay but not glad

Some homosexual teenagers feel proud and positive about being gay. Others feel depressed or guilty and wish that they could be like their straight friends. Accepting that you might be gay can be hard because the mainstream of society is straight and many straight people are homophobic i.e. they have strong anti-gay feelings. If you've realized that you're gay and you're feeling scared or depressed, here are a few positive things to bear in mind:

You're not alone. There are lesbians and gay men in all walks of life, in all parts of the world and from all racial and social groups.

Being proud to be gay in a heterosexual world takes guts, but this bravery can make you a stronger, more self-aware person.

Many young people panic when they realize for sure that they are gay. These negative feelings usually go away, however, when they talk about their feelings to supportive friends and meet new people with whom they might have a relationship.

Healthy, happy relationships are based on mutual love, affection and trust and that combination of goodies can be enjoyed by gay couples as well as straight.

You may have an advantage over your straight friends in that, because you know your own body and what turns you on, you may well know instinctively what turns your lover on.

I must have been 15 or 16 when I first realized I was gay. I came out at 17 – first, to my mother, who didn't mind: in fact, she said it was no surprise to her. It took a bit longer with my father; I was just talking to him, and mentioned some male relationships, and he had kind of accepted it by then: he said he'd gathered I was gay.

At school, I made up my mind that I'd come out when I found someone who'd come out to me as well. I felt I needed the support of one other person who was also gay. In the end, there was this lesbian friend who came out to me and then I felt I could talk to her about me. After that, I just came out to people I wanted to tell – I guess I was lucky in the friends I had. Most of them were girls or women. In fact, in my experience, straight females take it better than males.

My lesbian friend knew about the London Lesbian and Gay Switchboard, which gives advice, and a gay youth group, which we went to together. That was really good and empowering: it was the first time I'd been in all gay company, with other people who felt the same as me, where it was no big deal – it was a really nice feeling. I hadn't actually had a relationship till a few weeks ago, when I started going out with Josh, and that was magic.

(Dominic, 18)

Coming out

Acknowledging that you are gay to others is called coming out. Coming out can be a wonderfully liberating thing to do. It can give you a new confidence and make you feel like you are accepted for who you really are. Coming out may also cause friends and family to turn their backs on you, so it pays to assess your own situation carefully before you decide to take the plunge and come out. It also pays to talk the whole thing through with someone sensible, perhaps a gay friend you know well and trust or someone who works for your local Lesbian and Gay Switchboard. Look in the phone book for their number or try one of the numbers at the back of this book. There are also a number of books and leaflets available, written for lesbians and gay men, which include information and advice about coming out. Ask your local lesbian and gay information service which ones they would recommend.

Coming out to your parents

You don't have to tell your parents that you are gay, but many gay people who do find that their relationship with their parents improves because it is based on shared honesty and trust. If you are thinking about whether or not to come out to your parents, ask yourself the questions below. Your answers may help you make up your mind.

ARE YOU SURE YOU'RE GAY?

Coming out is not a good idea if you're unsure about your gay sexuality. The more confused you appear, the less confident your parents will be about your ability to know what you really want.

DO YOU FEEL POSITIVE ABOUT BEING GAY?

Coming out can be a traumatic experience, but if you feel positive about yourself and are able to face the whole thing with courage and dignity, you'll increase your chances of success.

WHY DO YOU WANT TO COME OUT TO YOUR PARENTS?

Coming out to your parents because you love them and want to be more honest with them is fine. Coming out to them during an argument or to 'get back' at them in some way is never a good idea.

HOW WELL DO YOU GET ON WITH YOUR PARENTS?

If you know that you and your parents love each other and you think that one or both will be understanding, there is a good chance that they will be able to deal with your news positively, even if their acceptance takes some time.

CAN YOU SUPPORT YOURSELF FINANCIALLY?

If you think that your parents will react so badly to your news that they might stop supporting you financially or throw you out of their house, you might want to wait until you are financially independent. (If you know that your parents are horribly homophobic and would probably throw you out of the house if they found out about your love life, be sensible. Don't leave love-letters, poems, unlocked diaries or any other dead give-aways lying around for them to find by accident.)

DO YOU HAVE SOMEONE TO TURN TO?

If your parents' reaction to your news is hurtful, you'll need someone you can turn to for comfort and support. If you don't have a friend or relation who you can turn to, you could strike up contact with someone from a gay helpline before you share your news.

If you have already come out to a sympathetic member of your family, you might find it helpful to have them around when you tell your parents.

WHAT ARE YOUR PARENTS' RELIGIOUS OR MORAL VIEWS?

If your parents believe that homosexuality is a sin, they may have a major problem accepting your sexuality. That's not to say they will stop loving you. They just may not be able to accept your sexuality, and you can't force someone to accept something that they don't want to. (If religion is important to you, there are a number of gay religious groups which you can contact such as The Lesbian and Gay Christian Movement – see pages 188.) If, however, your parents have shown some flexibility about other moral and social matters in the past, they may be able to come to terms with your sexuality in time.

HOW STRESSED ARE THINGS AT HOME?
If things are uneasy at home because, for example, one of your parents is depressed, worried or ill, you'd be better off holding on to your news until things are less fraught.

DO YOU HAVE ANY RESOURCE MATERIAL TO GIVE YOUR PARENTS?
Giving your parents a book for parents with gay children when you come out can help no end, even if your parents refuse to read it straight away. Good books include *A Stranger in the Family ... how to cope if your child is gay* by Terry Sanderson, published by The Other Way Press, 1991. Alternatively, have the telephone number of a parents-of-gays support group, or the name and telephone number of a non-gay counsellor, to hand when you share your news. Your parents may be glad of them. You'll find some crucial contacts on pages 182-190.

ARE YOU CLUED UP ABOUT SAFER SEX AND HOMOSEXUALITY?
Your parents may be worried about you catching HIV, the virus which can lead to AIDS. Therefore the more clued-up you are about safer sex, the easier you'll find it to reassure them that you are aware of the risks and know how to reduce them. Reading and learning about homosexuality in general may help, too. That way you'll be able to correct any anti-gay myths your parents may come out with.

ARE YOU PREPARED TO BE PATIENT?

Some parents need months, if not a couple of years, to reach a point where they can truly accept their child's sexuality. Although you may find this insulting, you'll be more successful if you are prepared to give yours all the time and space they need.

WHOSE DECISION IS IT?

You should only come out if you think you'll be the one to benefit by doing this. There is no rule which says you have to come out to your parents, so don't be pressurized into sharing your news if you don't want to.

'I haven't told my parents. I think they may know, but don't want to talk about it.'
(Narinder, 18)

A parents'-eye view of coming out

Not surprisingly, different parents react in different ways to the news that their child is gay. For some, the news is no big surprise because they've been expecting it for ages. For others, the news is like a bolt from the blue and they need a lot of time, sometimes years, to deal with it positively.

'My mum wanted to chuck me out when I told her. But she's finally realized it doesn't change anything: I'm still me.'
(Andreas, 18)

Below you'll find a selection of the different emotional responses gay children have faced from their parents, plus some suggestions for ways in which you could respond if you are faced with these responses yourself. Needless to say, there is no guarantee that your parents will experience all of these responses in this order, so be prepared for different reactions.

'It's like you've died!'

If your parents had absolutely no idea you are gay, their first reaction may be shock. This can last from minutes to days. The best thing you can do if shock has set in is to remind your parents that you are the same person you were before you broke the news and tell them that you love them. Keep on reminding them of your love, even if it looks as though your words are falling on deaf ears. You can only hope that in time your words will sink in.

'You can't be gay ... it's just a phase'

Many people react to shocking news by refusing to accept what they have heard. 'I don't want to know!', 'You're too pretty/masculine to be gay', 'You'll get over it', 'It's so-and-so's (i.e. your partner's) fault. *You're* not really gay' are not unusual reactions. Nor are complete silence, crying, screaming or shouting.

However badly your parents react, try and stay cool, calm and confident. If they tell you it's just a phase you're going through, let them know gently but firmly that it's not a phase as far as you're concerned. If they think that being gay is not normal, let them know that being gay is normal for you. If your parents tell you that they don't want to talk about what you've said, don't let the matter drop. Wait a week or so, choose a time when they're feeling relaxed and gently and sensitively try to talk to them again. Tell them that you're happy to talk to them about your sexuality whenever they're ready to do so, but don't give them lots of details that they don't need to know such as what you and your partner get up to in bed.

If you think it would help, suggest to your parents that they see a counsellor who isn't gay.

'Where did we go wrong?'

Some parents feel that they are to blame for their child's homosexuality. If your parents take a guilt trip, it may help to let them know that no one is certain why some people are gay and as far as you are concerned your sexual preference is nobody's fault. Once again, giving your parents an appropriate book to read or the phone number of a parents-of-gays support group may help. If you know someone who your parents respect and who is sympathetic to your case, you could suggest that your parents talk to that person, too. Don't be disappointed if your parents don't respond to your suggestions immediately. They may do in time.

'Why are you punishing us?'

At some stage your parents will probably start talking about how they feel about your sexuality. This may be a hard time for you, particularly if the feelings expressed are anger, hurt, or disappointment. Parents often react strongly in these ways for a number of reasons. Some feel they've been denied the chance to have grandchildren. Others worry that being gay will make life harder for their child. In these risky times many panic about their child getting AIDS, too. Whatever their reaction, let your parents have their say, and in the case of HIV and AIDS, let them know that you are clued up about the dangers (see Chapter 7 for information on HIV, AIDS and other sexually transmitted infections). If your parents say that they can't understand your homosexuality, try and help them see that they don't need to understand it, they only need to accept it. If your parents say that they can't cope with the thought of you sleeping with your gay lover, tell them gently that they don't need to think about it. After all, most people don't really want or like to think of their relations in sexual situations. They just accept that it happens and leave it at that. If your parents try to make you feel guilty for coming out in the first place, try and remain strong and positive about yourself. You are not responsible for their broken expectations, or feelings of guilt or shame.

'OK. It's decision-time'

At some point your parents will make a decision about how they are going to 'deal' with your sexuality long-term. Chances are that they will (1) accept the situation and be supportive; or (2) they will make it clear that they have gone as far as they wish to go with regard to 'accepting' your sexuality and they don't want to discuss it any further; or (3) they will continue to feel angry and use your sexuality as a weapon to criticize anything you do which they don't like.

If your parents choose option (1), you will probably find that your relationship with them improves brilliantly. Some caring parents even go so far as to campaign for gay and lesbian causes.

If they go for option (2), try and respect their wishes but don't withdraw from them. Let them know how important they are to you and slowly introduce them to some of your gay friends. Once they see that your pals are no more bizarre or depraved than anyone else, they may start to feel less prejudiced about homosexuality.

If they opt for option (3) and they can't be persuaded to chat about your homosexuality with a sensible, helpful non-homophobic adult, you may need to find yourself a trustworthy, supportive adult whom you can turn to for comfort and advice. If you don't have a friend or relation who fits the bill, there are lots of helpful contacts at the back of this book.

Coming out to your school mates

Deciding whether or not to come out to your friends at school can be tricky. Being gay isn't exactly a curriculum subject and some teenagers, like some adults, are very narrow-minded when it comes to homosexuality. If you are thinking of coming out to a friend at school, consider the advice in 'Coming Out to Your Parents', with, of course, the obvious modifications. If you can, ask some gay adults what coming out was like for them at school, too. Their experiences may help you decide what you should or shouldn't do. If you don't want to chat to an adult or ring a Helpline, think about sussing out your friends before you tell them, to see what their views about gays and lesbians really are. If you decide to open up but don't want the whole school to know your business, make sure you only confide in people you can really trust.

Many gay people who come out to their straight friends find that these friends are completely fine about the news, as well they should be. Others find that some of their so-called friends tease or reject them. If the latter situation happens to you, remember that they are the ones with the problem, not you. Besides, if that is how your friends react when you share something that important with them, you're better off without them.

Making new friends
One of the best ways to meet new friends who are in a similar position to yourself is to join a gay youth or social club, or to go to a gay pub, club or café. You can find out about your nearest social group or pub etc. from your local Lesbian and Gay Switchboard. Local listing magazines and gay magazines and papers may also have news about gay groups, places and events near you.

'My advice to anyone would be, don't be afraid to come out. It's surprising: sometimes people I've thought would reject me, or maybe even get rough, have said, "Oh, thank God, I am too." It's much better when you're out.'
(Keely, 17)

Chapter 6

sex

CONTRACEPTION

How pregnancy happens

Every time a lad ejaculates, or 'comes', millions of sperm are squirted out of the end of his stiff penis. If he ejaculates inside a girl's vagina or even inside the lips around her vaginal opening, the sperm can swim up her vagina and into her uterus. If just one of these sperm joins up with an egg released from the girl's ovaries, the girl will become pregnant. (If you've forgotten where the uterus and ovaries are in the female body, see page 27.)

A girl's ovaries usually release one egg each month. If the egg doesn't meet up with a sperm it disintegrates after a day or so and leaves the girl's body with her period blood. This means that there are only a few days each month when a girl can get pregnant. Unfortunately the time an egg is released can vary from month to month and most girls have no idea exactly when this happens. What's more, sperm can live inside a girl's body for up to five days – a few have been known to survive for a staggering eight days – so even if there isn't an egg there to meet the sperm when they first arrive, one may appear before they die off. In other words, it's hard to know when a sperm and an egg might meet. So, if you and your partner want to 'go the whole way' but you don't want to be parents yet, it's vital that you use some form of contraception to stop any sperm reaching an egg.

FACT: Sperm don't hang about. They travel at an average speed of about 3 mm per minute, and they can reach a girl's egg in under half an hour.

There are a lot of old wives' tales about how to prevent a pregnancy without using contraception. You may have heard it said that a girl can't get pregnant if ... it's her first time *or* she does it standing up *or* she does it before her first period *or* she does it during her period *or* she has a bath or wee afterwards *or* she doesn't have an orgasm *or* she washes her vagina out, or douches, afterwards *or* her boyfriend pulls his penis out of her vagina before he comes *or* her boyfriend doesn't put it in all the way.

Don't believe any of these 'tales'. *They are all a load of old cobblers!* The following points, however, are true:

> ▶ Scary though it may seem, a girl can get pregnant before her first period. This is because during her first menstrual cycle, her ovaries may release an egg days before she starts to bleed. If a sperm reaches this egg, she'll get pregnant.
>
> ▶ Although it is unusual, a girl can also get pregnant during her period because an egg can be released unexpectedly early or late.
>
> ▶ Douching, or washing out the vagina, can push sperm further up the vagina – which is bad news if the girl is trying to prevent a pregnancy.
>
> ▶ The 'withdrawal method' which involves a lad pulling his penis out of a girl's vagina before he ejaculates is an extraordinarily unreliable attempt at contraception. This is because men often ejaculate a tiny bit of semen before the main spurt, and if this little bit of semen gets inside the vagina, the girl could get pregnant.

FACT: In some tribal cultures men repeatedly dip their testicles in very hot water over several days before having sex in order to kill off the sperm and so stop their women from becoming pregnant. This is not, however, a reliable method of birth control.

Front line contraceptives

As you probably know, there are a number of good reliable methods of birth control on offer in the UK today. However, not all these methods reduce the risk of catching sexually transmitted infections, or STIs for short. One method of contraception which **does** help protect against unplanned pregnancy **and** STIs, including HIV, the virus that can lead to AIDS, is the condom. In fact, using a condom carefully is the **only** way to reduce the risk of catching HIV during penetrative sex. So unless you and your partner are 100 per cent sure that neither of you is infected with any type of sexually transmitted disease, it's essential that you use a condom each and every time you make love. (For more information about HIV infection and other sexually transmitted infections, see Chapter 7).

I didn't put any pressure on my girlfriend to go on to full-scale sex, I didn't say anything. We went on for about five months, and then one time we were heavy petting and I thought, 'Let's do it.' I always had a condom: I had always thought, I'd use a condom if we get to that, becoming a father is not something I want at this stage: it would put a hell of a strain on our lives and relationship, no matter how much we love each other.
(Tom, 17)

105

Male condoms
aka (also known as)

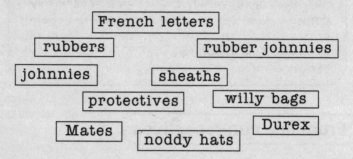

French letters

rubbers   rubber johnnies

johnnies   sheaths

protectives   willy bags

Mates   Durex
        noddy hats

Male condoms are soft, stretchy tubes, made from latex rubber or polyurethane, which are closed at one end like the finger of a glove. They fit snugly onto a penis when it's stiff and they keep semen in and other body fluids out.

Advantages: They are easy to get hold of; easy to put on by either partner; easy to carry around; make sex a lot less messy; help protect both partners from a number of sexually transmitted infections, including HIV, the virus that can lead to AIDS.

Disadvantages: They can split or come off if not put on properly, or if the vagina isn't wet enough; putting one on may interrupt sex.

The failure rate of the male spermicidally-lubricated condom when used properly, according to instructions is about two per cent. That means of every 100 women using a condom properly two will get pregnant in a year. If condoms are not used according to instructions, their failure rate increases.

Condoms complaints

Although male condoms have a lot going for them, some men kick up a fuss about wearing them because they claim that condoms make the penis feel less sensitive. Others complain that no condom is big enough to wear comfortably. And, as you've just read, both sexes sometimes find putting on a condom interrupts sex. However, the truth of the matter is that if you want to protect yourself from HIV as well as other sexually transmitted infections during penetrative sex, you have no choice but to use a condom. Besides, wearing a condom doesn't make that much difference to how sex feels – modern condoms are thinner than those of old and putting one on is quick and hassle-free once you've got the hang of it. As for size ... condoms are available in a variety of sizes and a standard-sized one can stretch to fit over a fist!

'Nice girls' and condoms

Unbelievable though it may seem, some young women don't like carrying condoms because they think that 'nice girls' don't expect or plan to have sex. PLEASE!! Just because a girl, nice or not, decides to carry a packet of condoms around with her, doesn't mean that her morals are looser than a pair of baggy pants. Lots of women, like lots of men, carry condoms around with them not because they're on the hunt for sex, but because they value their good health and don't ever want to wind up in a situation where they want to have sex but don't have a condom.

FACT: In Victorian times the English called condoms 'French letters' and the French called them 'capotes anglaise' which means English hoods.

How to use a condom

Condoms are sold in packets. Inside, each condom comes rolled up in a small foil-lined sachet. To use a condom:

Wait for the penis to go hard and then carefully tear one corner of the sachet, using both thumbs and forefingers, and slide out the condom. Don't bite open the sachet or rip it apart like a rhino on heat. Condoms are strong, but they can be torn by sharp fingernails, teeth or jewellery.

Once you've got the condom out of its sachet, place it over the end of the penis with the roll on the outside. Gently squeeze the teat or closed end between your thumb and forefinger. This squeezes out any trapped air and makes room for the semen. Keep holding the closed end and, using your other hand, roll the condom right down the penis. If uncircumcised, pull back the foreskin before rolling on the condom.

If the condom won't roll down properly, chances are you've put it on inside out. Pull it off and start again with a new condom.

Only put on the condom when the penis is stiff and hard, and long before it goes anywhere near a vagina or anus. A tiny amount of semen often leaks out of a penis when it first becomes hard, and that tiny bit of sperm-filled semen could be enough to pass on a sexually transmitted infection (an STI) or make a girl pregnant.

The condom may come off during sex, if the penis stops being 100 per cent stiff. Feel around the base of the penis every now and then to check that the rim of the condom is still there. If it is, you're OK! If it's not, quickly unroll the condom back into place. If it comes off completely, stop and put on a new one before you go any further.

It is important to withdraw the penis from the vagina soon after ejaculation, while it is still hard. Hold the rim of the condom tightly to the penis as you do this, to stop the condom from slipping off and to help stop any semen from spilling out.

When the penis is completely withdrawn, remove the condom carefully, wrap it up in a tissue and put it in a dustbin (not down the toilet). Whatever you do, don't try and use the condom again. Each condom should be used once and once only!

Like many things in life, putting on a condom gets easier the more practice you have, so don't wait until you're having sex for the first time to learn how to put one on. Be bold and practise beforehand! If you've got a penis, you could try putting a condom on when you masturbate. If you haven't got a penis, practise putting a condom on a banana, cucumber or any other penis-shaped object you can lay your hands on.

Condom shopping

In the UK you can buy condoms from all sorts of places including chemists, supermarkets, petrol stations and slot machines in pubs, clubs and other places with public toilets. Don't feel embarrassed about buying your own condoms. Lots of people, young and old, buy them every day without so much as batting an eyelid.

You can also get condoms free from some family planning clinics, some sexual health clinics and Brook Advisory Centres. For information on where to find your nearest clinic or centre turn to page 182. A number of family doctors or GPs also supply free male condoms, as do some HIV and AIDS services. Members of both sexes are welcome at clinics either on their own or with a partner and you don't need your parents' permission to talk to whoever you see. (See page 168 for details about your rights to confidential birth control advice and supplies.)

In the UK many packets of condoms have a heart-shaped symbol on them surrounded by the words 'Certified To British Standard', and/or the letters CE. These are the best condoms to buy.

Condoms don't last for ever which is why every condom packet should have an expiry date printed on it. If this is out of date, don't buy the packet. Similarly if the expiry date printed on a condom sachet is long gone, or if the sachet is split, don't use the condom inside.

Finally, to keep your condoms in tiptop condition, store them away from heat, sunlight or damp.

Choosing a condom

Condoms come in an awesome array of colours, shapes and flavours, including curry flavour! There are even some novelty ones that glow in the dark! (Many novelty condoms, however, cannot be relied on for protection against unwanted pregnancy or infection.) If you're confused as to what's what on the condom counter, here's a run-down of the main types on offer:

Spermicidally-lubricated condoms Many condoms are covered with a substance called spermicide which contains an ingredient called nonoxynol-9. Nonoxynol-9 is great stuff because it is capable of destroying sperm and killing most STIs.* Spermicide also makes a good lubricant. That

*Spermicides containing nonoxynol-9 have been shown in laboratory tests to kill STIs including HIV. However, spermicide on its own or used with a diaphragm (see page 116) is not thought to offer good protection against HIV. Nor will the spermicide on a condom offer enough protection against pregnancy if the condom splits.

means it helps a penis slide in and out of a vagina more easily (see page 113 for more about lubricants).

Wonderful though it is, nonoxynol-9 can cause soreness in a few people. If you have a bad reaction to spermicidally-lubricated condoms, switch to a non-spermicidally lubricated brand and see if that helps.

Non-spermicidally-lubricated condoms These condoms are just the ticket for anyone who is allergic to spermicide.

Flavoured condoms These condoms are designed to make oral sex more tasty. (Lick a regular condom coated in spermicide by mistake and you'll soon see why flavoured condoms are on the market!) Not all flavoured condoms are strong enough for vaginal sex though, so always check the packet.

Ribbed condoms Unlike regular straight-sided condoms, these have thin raised hoops running down the length of the condom, which are designed to make the vagina extra tingly. Some girls love them, but others don't think they make any difference at all.

Super thin/ultra fine condoms These condoms are ideal for lads who complain that their penis doesn't feel very sensitive in a condom. Extra thin condoms are fine, but they aren't good for rough or anal sex as they aren't as strong as other condoms on the market. Most extra fine condoms are made from latex rubber, but there is now a brand on the market made from polyurethane.

Extra/ultra strong/thick condoms No condoms have been tested for anal sex, but extra strong ones are the toughest on the market and therefore the safest ones to use for this type of sex. Many people put extra lubrication on the outside of the condom (see page 113) to help stop it from tearing.

Extra strong condoms can, of course, be used for vaginal sex as well as anal sex. They are also useful for any lad who wants to keep his erection longer because they cut down on sensations.

The female condom
aka (also known as)

> Femidom

In recent years a new type of condom, designed to be worn by women, has come onto the market. This female condom looks like a big unrolled male condom with a flexible ring at each end. The smaller ring is used to push the condom up inside the vagina and keep it in place. The larger ring which is around the opening of the condom stays outside the body. Like the male condom, the female variety stops sperm getting inside the girl's body and so helps

112

protect against infection and pregnancy. Unlike most male condoms, however, the female one is made of see-through polyurethane and has a slippery coating on the inside.

Advantages: It can be put in place at any time during sex, but before genital contact; can be taken out of the vagina at any time after a sex session finishes; helps protect against various sexually transmitted infections as well as unwanted pregnancy.

Disadvantages: You have to check that the penis goes inside the condom and not between the condom and the vagina; putting one in can interrupt sex; may slip; some men complain that a female condom is like having sex with a plastic bag, although how many of these men have actually had sex with a plastic bag, it's best not to speculate.

> The failure rate of the female condom when used properly is thought to be about five per cent. If condoms are not used according to instructions, their failure rate increases.

Female condom shopping

You can buy female condoms from chemists and super-markets or you can get them free from some sexual health and family planning clinics. Each box comes with instructions. If you find the instructions hard to follow, ask your nearest Brook Advisory Centre or youth advisory clinic to show you what to do.

Luscious lube

The vagina is naturally smooth and slippery, but sometimes it needs a little more slipperiness, or lubrication, to make penetrative sex more comfortable. The anus isn't naturally lubricated so it needs all the help it can get. This is where slippery oils or gels called lubricants come in handy. Lubricants, or lubes for short, can be bought in chemists or got free from family planning clinics or Brook Advisory Centres. If you decide to use a lube for penetrative sex, make sure you put it inside the vagina or anus, or on the outside of a male condom or on the inside of a female condom. If you are using latex rubber condoms make sure the lube you buy is water-based, too. Oil-based products, such as petroleum jelly, baby oil, butter, massage oil and lipstick can damage the latex rubber used to make most male condoms*. So too can some medications designed to go in or around your genital area. If you are using such medication, ask your doctor or pharmacist whether they will affect a condom.

If you decide to invest in some lube, remember that you don't have to use it just for penetrative sex. Smoothing a squirt of lube on to your partner's private parts before you masturbate them will more than double their delight!

Your condom or mine?

Using a condom for the first time with someone needn't be embarrassing. The secret is to raise the subject before you both get so carried away that you can't think or talk coolly. In other words, have a chat about using condoms with your partner before either of you is really turned on or too tired. Don't wait for

*Polyurethane condoms can be used with oil and water-based lubricants.

your partner to bring the subject up because that may never happen. If you really can't chat to your partner in advance, pick a moment before things get too physical and then say something like 'Have you got a condom?' or 'Shall I go and get my condoms?' Be as straightforward as you can and if your partner won't agree to using a condom, don't have penetrative sex with them! Having sex without a condom is not just risky infections-wise. It also shows that you don't respect yourself enough to protect your health. And if you don't respect yourself, why should anyone else?

Sex and drugs and alcohol

Most people feel a lot less shy about sex once they've got some alcohol inside them. But sex and alcohol, like sex and drugs, can be a terrible combination. Firstly, too much alcohol can make the stiffest of penises droop. And secondly, getting drunk or stoned can make you forget about using a condom – which is something you may live to regret.

Back-up contraception

Condoms are great because they help provide protection against STIs as well as pregnancy. However, as you have now discovered, they are not 100 per cent reliable, even when used carefully. This means that if you and your partner want maximum protection against pregnancy as well as protection against STIs, you'd be wise to use a condom **and** another method of birth control as a back-up to the condom.

Women's work?

All the methods of contraception available these days, except the male condom and male sterilization, are designed to be used by females. But this doesn't mean that contraception is solely a girl's responsibility. After all, it takes two to make a pregnancy and the more support a lad gives his girlfriend in helping her to choose and use back-up birth control, the more relaxed they'll both be about the sex they share. That said, however, the final say about which method of back-up contraception to use should go to the girl, as she will be the one using it.

Contraception contacts

The following basic information about contraception, which is mainly aimed at female readers, is just for starters. A GP, family planning clinic, Brook Advisory Centre or young people's clinic will give you further details about the pros and cons of each method, help you decide which method is right for you and hopefully give you what you need – all for free. Not all the methods will suit everyone, so be prepared to tell the doctor or nurse about your own and your family's medical history.

If you are over 16 (over 17 in Northern Ireland) it is legal for you to have sex, so you should have no trouble getting contraceptives from a doctor without your parents'/guardians' consent. If you are under 16 it is not legal for you to be having sex, so it is up to the doctor you see whether s/he gives you the contraceptives you want without parental consent (see page 168 for more details).

The diaphragm with spermicide

A diaphragm is a small, rubber bowl with a bendy rim. You cover part of it with spermicide and then push it up into your vagina, over your cervix, so that it forms a barrier to stop sperm from reaching an egg. To be truly effective the diaphragm must stay inside your vagina for at least six hours after sex. You can leave it in place longer but you should never wear it for more than 24 hours at a time.

Vaginas vary in size so you need to get a doctor or nurse to fit you out with a diaphragm, and to show you how to use it.

Advantages It can be put in any time before you have vaginal sex (if you put it in more than three hours before, you'll have to add some extra spermicide); has no serious health risks; may help protect against cancer of the cervix and cervical infections; only needs to be used when you want to have sex; can be used to catch your period blood if you want to have sex when you're 'on'.

Disadvantages: Putting it in may interrupt sex; more spermicide is needed if you have sex more than three hours after you put the diaphragm in and/or if you have sex more than once in one session; the fit needs checking every 6-12 months and if you gain or lose more than 3kg in weight, or if you have a baby, miscarriage or abortion; some girls get urinary tract infections, but changing to a different type or size of diaphragm can help; some girls or their partners get sore from the spermicide, but using a different brand may help; does not protect against some STIs.

Remember: Spermicide on its own is not a reliable method of birth control.

> **Like condoms, how well a diaphragm with spermicide works depends on how well it is used. The failure rate of the diaphragm when used properly, according to instructions is about four to eight per cent.**

> **FACT:** One form of contraception which never took off in a big way was 'The Human Birth Control Appliance'. This contraceptive which was patented in 1970 was like a pair of knickers with an expandable crotch. The idea was that the crotch would be pushed up into the vagina during penetrative sex and form a barrier to stop sperm from reaching the uterus.

The IUD
aka (also known as)

> the coil

> the intra-uterine device

The IUD is a small plastic and copper T-shaped device with two threads hanging from the end of it. It fits inside your uterus (the threads hang out through your cervix) and it works mainly by stopping sperm from meeting an egg.

The IUD must be fitted by a doctor but once inserted, it can be left in place for about five years. It is not usually given to young women who are not in long-term relationships where both partners only have sex with each other. This is because IUD wearers who have more than one partner, or who are with a partner who has other lovers, are at risk of getting a sexually transmitted infection which could travel up into the uterus. For this reason, clinics should check whether you have an infection before they fit an IUD or IUS.

Advantages It is very reliable; works as soon as it is put in; only needs changing about every five years; doesn't interrupt sex in any way; easy to check that it's in place – if you can feel the threads with your fingers, all is OK.

Disadvantages It can cause heavier, longer or more painful periods; can come out without you noticing it; can occasionally go through your uterus or cervix when it is fitted; offers no protection from STIs; if you get pregnant there is a small risk that the pregnancy may implant in one of your Fallopian tubes instead of in your uterus. This is called an ectopic pregnancy and it is a major problem.

> The failure rate of the IUD is less than two per cent.

118

The IUS
aka (also known as)

intra-uterine system

The IUS is a small T-shaped plastic device which contains a progestogen hormone. It is fitted into the uterus by a doctor or nurse and it works mainly by thickening the mucus in your cervix so that no sperm can swim through and by making the lining of your uterus too thin to support a fertilized egg.

Advantages It is very reliable; works as soon as it is put in; can be left in place for at least three years; makes periods shorter and lighter and less painful.

Disadvantages It may produce temporary side-effects such as breast soreness and acne; can cause irregular bleeding in the first three months; can come out without you noticing it; can occasionally go through your uterus or cervix when it is fitted; offers no protection from STIs.

The failure rate of the IUS is less than one per cent.

The Pill
aka (also known as)

the combined pill

oral contraception

the progestogen only pill (POP)

There are two main types of contraceptive pill – the combined pill and progestogen-only pill (aka POP). The first you take once a day for three weeks out of every four and you have a 'period' in the fourth week. The other you take at the same time every day without a break. The combined pill works mainly by stopping your ovaries from releasing an egg each month. The progestogen-only pill works by thickening the mucus from your cervix which makes it difficult for sperm to reach an egg. It also thins the lining of your uterus so that a fertilized egg stands less chance of sticking to it. In some women the POP stops an egg from being released at all.

The contraceptive pill is available from most GPs, family planning clinics, young people's clinics or Brook Advisory Centres.

Advantages It is easy to use (provided you remember to take it when you are supposed to); very effective; doesn't interrupt sex; the combined pill makes periods less painful and reduces the risk of cancer of the ovaries and uterus and protects you against some pelvic infections.

Disadvantages It may bring on temporary side-effects such as headaches, breast tenderness, weight gain and feeling sick – occasionally the side-effects from the combined pill are much more serious (for example, there is a small chance of developing a blood clot which can block a vein); doesn't protect from STIs; the POP may cause irregular periods or spotting; the combined pill is not reliable if you take it over 12 hours late; the POP is not reliable if taken over three hours late; neither pill is reliable if you vomit within three hours of taking your pill or if you have really bad diarrhoea; some medicines prescribed by a doctor or dentist, such as antibiotics, may stop the pill from working.

Women on the combined pill do have a statistically increased risk of having breast cancer diagnosed when they are on the pill, but the risk disappears over a ten-year period after they stop taking it. Research is ongoing in this area: it is also the case that, if you were to develop breast cancer, it would probably be diagnosed quicker because of the regular check-ups that pill users normally have.

Combined pill users should try not to smoke as smoking increases the risk of circulatory problems for women on the pill.

> **The failure rate of the combined pill is less than one per cent. The failure rate of the POP is one per cent.**

> **FACT:** In 1996 Brian McDonald became the first man in Britain to start testing the male contraceptive pill. According to Brian, the pill hasn't affected his sex drive one bit! If the male pill proves successful in trials, it could be available on prescription by the year 2000.

Contraceptive injections

There are two types of contraceptive injections. They are usually injected into your buttocks and work by releasing the hormone progestogen very slowly into your body. This stops you ovulating i.e. releasing an egg each month.

Advantages It is very effective; doesn't interrupt sex; one type of injection protects you against pregnancy for 12 weeks, the other protects you for eight weeks; may protect against cancer of the uterus.

121

Disadvantages Your periods will probably change; periods often become irregular or stop completely; regular periods and your ability to have a baby may take a year or more to return after you stop having the injections; can make you put on weight; may make you feel depressed; once it has been injected, the progestogen cannot be removed from your body so if you get unwanted side-effects you'll have to wait two or three months for the injection to wear off before they disappear; offers no protection from STIs.

> **The failure rate of contraceptive injections is less than one per cent.**

Contraceptive implants

The implant called Norplant is made up of six tiny soft tubes which contain a progestogen hormone. It is planted just under the skin in the inside of your upper arm by a doctor or nurse. The implant's capsules slowly release the hormone into your bloodstream. This makes the mucus at the entrance to your uterus too thick for sperm to get through to meet an egg.

Advantages These are very reliable; can be left in place (and will keep on providing contraceptive cover) for up to five years; this method doesn't interrupt sex.

Disadvantages Your periods will probably change; periods are often irregular during the first year; can cause side-effects such as headaches, sickness, acne and weight gain; removal of the implant is sometimes difficult; some medicines prescribed by a doctor make an implant less effective; offers no protection from STIs.

> **The failure rate of a contraceptive implant is less than one per cent in the first year of use. This rises to two per cent over five years.**

Natural family planning aka (also known as)

natural birth control

natural method

fertility awareness

This method of birth control helps you recognize the days in your menstrual cycle when you are most likely to get pregnant. You do this by keeping daily records of natural signs linked to your menstrual cycle such as changes in your body temperature and changes to the mucus from your vagina. You will need a natural family planning teacher to help you understand this method properly and it will probably take you about three to six months before you can understand your recordings well enough to use the method.

Advantages It doesn't interfere with the way your body works; has no physical side-effects; means both lovers take responsibility for contraception; makes a woman more aware of how her body works; makes it easier to plan when to get pregnant.

Disadvantages It takes a lot of time and commitment to make this method work; you can't have sex on your fertile days unless you use a condom or diaphragm; needs both lovers to be committed to the method (i.e. it works best for couples in a steady, long-term relationship); doesn't protect against STIs; events such as illness can make this method less reliable.

> The failure rate of natural family planning when used according to instructions is about two per cent.

PERSONA

PERSONA is the most recent of all the methods of contraception in this book. It works by measuring changes in the levels of the hormones in your body which control your monthly cycle. It is best suited to couples in long-term relationships and is available from leading pharmacies in the UK.

Each PERSONA starter pack contains a small Monitor, which would fit into a handbag, some special sticks for testing pee and an instructions booklet which you must read carefully. You have to wait until your period begins before you can start using the Monitor. Then you must check the Monitor each morning to see which of its coloured lights is shining. A yellow light means that you need to test your early morning pee with one of the test sticks. To do this, you hold the test stick in your stream of pee and then insert it into the Monitor. The Monitor then works out whether to give you a red or green light.

A green light means that you are unlikely to become pregnant if you have sex on that day. A red light means that you're at risk of becoming pregnant if you have sex on that day. Luckily, you don't need to do a pee test every day of the month because the Monitor can store plenty of information. In the first month of use you do 16 pee tests. After that you do eight a month.

Advantages There are no side-effects; doesn't interrupt love-making; easy to use provided you remember to check the Monitor each morning.

Disadvantages It is not available free from Family Planning Clinics etc; expensive to buy (in addition to the starter pack, you have to buy a box of test sticks every month); you have to do a pee test some mornings each month; need to use another form of back-up contraception if you want to have sex on your red light days; can only be used if your natural menstrual cycle lasts between 23 and 35 days; offers no protection from STIs; it can be less accurate if a person is taking certain medications, such as antibiotics for acne.

> **The failure rate of PERSONA when used properly is about six per cent.**

Sterilization
aka (also known as)

> tying the tubes

> female sterilization

> vasectomy (male sterilization)

A sterilization is an operation performed on a man or a woman which makes him/her sterile i.e. unable to have a baby. By and large, sterilization cannot be reversed, which means that you have to be 100 per cent sure that you don't ever want to have a child before you have the operation. It is unlikely that as a teenager

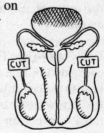

you would be offered sterilization as a choice of contraceptive even if you say that you never want children, because there is a strong possibility that you might change your mind in years to come.

> **The failure rate of male and female sterilization is almost zero.**

> **FACT:** Back in the eighteenth century honeysuckle juice was recommended by physicians as a male contraceptive. It was believed that if a man drank this juice for 37 days on the trot he would end up sterile.

Emergency contraception

If you have had sex without using any contraception, or you fear that your contraceptive method hasn't worked, there are two emergency forms of contraception you can use. One is the emergency Pill. The other is the emergency IUD.

The Pill is given in two doses. The first dose must be taken WITHIN 3 DAYS (72 hours) of having unprotected sex. The IUD must be fitted WITHIN 5 DAYS of unprotected sex.

Advantages Both methods are very reliable if taken/fitted on time.

Disadvantages The pill (which is much stronger than the combined pill) may make you feel sick or throw up (so it's best to take it after you've eaten); the IUD is not suitable for any woman or girl who is at risk of a sexually trans-mitted infection because the IUD may help spread the infection into the uterus (unless antibiotics are prescribed when the IUD is fitted).

> **The failure rate of the emergency pill is five per cent. The failure rate of the emergency IUD is less than one per cent.**

Emergency means emergency

Emergency contraceptives – which should be available from GPs, young people's and family planning clinics, some sexual health clinics, and some hospital accident and emergency departments (when you ring for an appointment, make it clear that you need to be seen quickly) – are for use in an emergency only. They are not as effective as using other methods of contraception regularly and for the minority of people the side-effects of the emergency pills, such as feeling sick and throwing up, can be horrible.

I've had to take the morning after pill [emergency pill] *twice: once when we had kind of unexpected sex – and neither of us said anything about precautions, contraception; maybe he thought I was on the pill. The other time, the condom split when we were making love, and we didn't notice till afterwards. I said, 'Oh God, I suppose I'll have to go to the clinic and get a morning after pill* [emergency pill].'

Andy was sweet, he came with me and waited at the clinic. The pill is horrible: it makes you feel really sick. You have to take it within 72 hours of unprotected sex, preferably one the night after, and one 12 hours later. If you chuck it up, you have to take another. It's best if you eat first. I took one at eight o'clock, the next one at eight in the morning, went back to sleep, then had

to get up later when I woke up feeling really ill and couldn't eat any breakfast.
(Helen, 17)

Contraception of the future

Sadly there is still no perfect method of contraception, so research is under way to improve existing methods and invent new ones. Who knows, by the time you read this you may be able to get hold of a contraceptive spray you squirt up your nose.

Chapter 7

sex

SEXUALLY
TRANSMITTED
INFECTIONS

Infectious love

A sexually transmitted infection, or STI for short, is an infection which is passed from one person to another during sex. In days gone by STIs were known as venereal diseases (VD for short) and more recently, sexually transmitted diseases (STDs for short). Many modern doctors now call them genito-urinary (or GU) infections. But whatever you choose to call them, one thing's for certain: most STIs are easily cured if they are treated early enough. If left untreated, however, some can cause serious long-term damage to your health.

> **FACT:** The term venereal disease comes from the Latin 'morbus venereus' which means the sickness of Venus. Venus was an ancient goddess of love.

STI alert!

There are lots of different types of sexually transmitted infection. General symptoms to look out for include:

▶ a discharge from your vagina, penis, pee-hole or anus which looks or smells unusual or unpleasant;

▶ pain or burning feeling when you pee;

▶ desire to pee very often or more often than usual for you;

▶ swollen private parts;

▶ pain when you have sex;

▶ pain low down in your tummy;

◗ bleeding between periods

◗ lumps, sores, warts or blisters on or near your private parts or anus;

◗ redness, itching or irritation around your private parts or anus;

◗ a horrid smell under your foreskin even when you wash regularly;

◗ blood in your pee;

◗ no symptoms at all!

> **If you own a pair of testicles and you suffer from a dull ache in them or notice blood coming from your penis or notice that one ball is growing heavier or larger than the other, get along to your doctor.**

Sexual healing

Scary though it may seem, it is possible to have a STI without having any obvious symptoms. This is because some STIs can remain in the body for months or years before they show any symptoms – which means that it is possible for you to be infected without knowing it and for you or your partner suddenly to develop symptoms of an infection which was picked up in an earlier relationship. So, if you have any reason to think you might have caught an infection, perhaps because a) you've had sex without using a condom, *or* b) you've had sex with someone who might have a STI, *or* c) you've developed any of the symptoms listed above, get down to your nearest sexual health clinic right away for a check-up. These clinics are also known as genito urinary medicine (GUM) clinics, sexually transmitted disease (STD) clinics, venereal disease (VD) clinics, special clinics or special treatment centres. To find your nearest one, look in the phone book under 'Clinics' or phone your nearest main hospital and ask. Alternatively you can call the Family Planning Association or the National AIDS helpline and ask them where your nearest clinic is.

Remember – if you think you may have caught a STI, even if you don't have any signs of the infection, it's vital that you get yourself checked out at a clinic as soon as possible, as the sooner you go for treatment, the quicker and simpler it will be for a doctor to help you. Take the STI chlamydia for example. This is the most common treatable bacterial STI in the West and if it is found early enough, it can be easily treated with a one week course of antibiotics. However, if it is left untreated it can cause pain and infertility.

The bacteria chlamydia, which is found in semen or vaginal fluids, can be passed on through vaginal, oral or anal sex. This means that it is possible for anyone who is sexually active to get chlamydia. However, the infection is most common in women under 25 and men under 30. Of those women with the infection, the majority will show no symptoms at all until the infection is far advanced. If all this sounds horribly bleak, take heart. Using a condom every time you have penetrative sex will reduce your risk of getting or passing on chlamydia; and getting treatment quickly if you suspect you've caught the infection or if you develop any of the first seven symptoms listed on page 131, should help speed you on the road to recovery.

If you suspect you've got chlamydia or any other STI, it's best not to have sex until the infection has been confirmed and you've had a course of treatment and been given the all-clear.

Going to a sexual health clinic

Going to a sexual health clinic is nothing to be red-faced about. STIs are common and thousands of people visit sexual health clinics each year. The staff at these clinics are used to looking at people's private parts and spotting sexual infections so you've no need to feel embarrassed about having an examination. What's more, the advice and treatment on offer is free and confidential – and you don't need a letter from your GP.

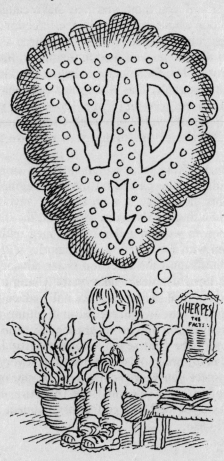

FACT: Getting the STI, syphilis, is hardly one of life's great pleasures, but in the fifteenth and sixteenth centuries the 'cure' for syphilis was almost as bad as the disease itself. In those days syphilitics were given mercury which often caused mouth ulcers, swollen gums, loosened teeth, bad breath and even death. Nowadays syphilis can be cured with a course of antibiotics!

Spreading the news

If a doctor confirms you've got an infection and suggests that you let your recent sexual partner/partners know about it, take note. No one likes having to tell someone that they may have an infection. But if you remember that you are doing your partner/ex-partners a big favour by letting them know that they may be carrying an infection without knowing, you should find the whole thing easier to deal with. If you really can't face breaking the news to your partner/ex-partners yourself, ask the health adviser for some advice.

HIV and AIDS

HIV infection, which can lead to AIDS, is not the most highly occurring illness in the UK, but like most people you've probably heard more about it than any other sexually transmitted infection because it is so serious. However, although there is a great deal of excellent literature around about HIV and AIDS, some people are still not properly clued-up about either. Nor are they clear what's risky HIV-wise and what's not. Just in case you are one of those people who is still a little unclear, here are some basic facts.

AIDS is short for acquired immune deficiency syndrome. It is caused by a type of virus, called HIV (human immuno-deficiency virus). People who have this virus in their body are called HIV positive.

HIV attacks and kills different cells in the body, including cells in the blood called T-helper cells. T-helper cells are needed to fight germs in the body. If the virus kills off too many T-helper cells the body's defence system is damaged, and unable to fight back against other germs which get into the body. When this happens the person becomes extremely ill, and is said to have AIDS. Sadly there is, as yet, no cure for HIV or AIDS.

> **FACT**: HIV was discovered by scientists in 1981. Up to December 1996, 6.4 million people around the world have died of AIDS.

How do you get HIV?

HIV survives in body fluids such as blood, semen, vaginal juices and breast milk. To get the virus, body fluids from an infected person have to enter your bloodstream. This can happen in three main ways:

▶ by sharing drug injection equipment with someone who is infected with HIV;

▶ from an HIV positive woman to her baby either before or during birth or through breast-feeding;

▶ through having vaginal or anal sex with an infected person without using a condom.

HIV cannot travel through the air like the germs that cause colds and flu. Nor can it pass through healthy undamaged skin. Nor can you get HIV infection by using cups, cutlery or toilet seats etc. that an HIV positive person has used.

HIV can get into the bloodstream during sex in a number of ways. The delicate skin inside a vagina can have tiny cuts in it. If semen infected with HIV gets into the cuts, the virus will go into the woman's bloodstream. The skin on a penis can also have tiny cuts on it. If infected period blood and/or vaginal juices get inside these cuts, or inside the hole at the tip of the penis, the man is at risk. Anal sex is particularly dodgy because the anal passage is less wet and stretchy than a vagina and so tears quite easily when a penis is put in it. During anal sex the penis can also get extra tears, which means that blood from the anal passage can pass through the tears into the penis's bloodstream.

Risky sex

Any sexual activity which allows semen, blood (including period blood) or vaginal juices to pass from one person into the body of another is classed as high risk as far as HIV is concerned. These activities include anal and vaginal sex without the use of a condom and withdrawing an unprotected penis from a vagina or anus before ejaculation takes place. Withdrawing the penis before its owner 'comes' is no safeguard against passing on infection because a tiny bit of semen often leaks out of a penis long before the main spurt ... and this little bit of semen may be infected.

HIV can also be transmitted by performing oral sex on, or receiving oral sex from someone infected by HIV – particularly if the person performing the deed has bleeding gums, or cuts, ulcers or infections in their mouth or throat. That said, the number of reported cases of people catching HIV through oral sex alone is few. Licking and sucking a penis seems to carry more risk than licking and sucking a vulva, because there is less virus in vaginal fluids than in semen, which is why people who want to play more safely use a flavoured condom when they perform oral sex on a man.

> **FACT:** A girl who is HIV positive is more likely to pass on the virus during sex when she is on her period because there is more HIV in period blood than in normal vaginal fluids.

Hugging, stroking, fondling, dancing naked, fingering with short unjagged nails etc. are all safe HIV-wise provided that no semen, vaginal juices or blood get into any broken skin or get transferred to any bodily opening by hand etc. Sharing sex toys, such as vibrators and dildos, is OK too provided that a new condom is put on the toy for each person, or the toy is washed between uses in soapy water. Remember to remove and dispose of any condoms you use carefully.

How do I know if I am HIV positive?

Many people who are HIV positive have no idea that they have the virus. They look, feel and believe that they are fit and well. It is only if they go on to develop AIDS (and many do) that they become obviously ill. In other words, you can't tell whether someone is HIV positive just by looking at them.

If you are worried that you have HIV, the only way you can find out is to have an HIV blood test. Most sexual health clinics offer the test. Do not go to your GP for the test.

Having an HIV test is not something you should undertake lightly, so it's important to talk through the pros and cons of having the test first, either with someone on the end of a Helpline (see pages 182–190 for some useful numbers) or a health adviser at your local sexual health clinic. The Terrence Higgins Trust also produce a useful booklet on HIV testing.

How to protect your partner and yourself from HIV and other sex-related infections.

Here are some important tips.

▶ Use a condom **each and every time** you have vaginal or anal sex. This is the only way you can lessen the risk of getting infected with HIV through these activities. Using condoms will also cut down your risk of catching other STIs, such as gonorrhoea, chlamydia and genital herpes simplex. (A diaphragm can help protect a girl's cervix from certain infections too). Keeping the number of sexual partners you have to a minimum will also lessen your risk of having sex with someone with a STI.

▶ Follow the advice for avoiding HIV infection given in 'Risky Sex' above. Don't let blood, semen or vaginal juices get into any broken skin or body orifice or opening. If your partner is male and you want to practise mouth-to-penis sex, use a flavoured condom.

▶ If your partner is a girl and you want to practise mouth-to-vulva sex as safely as possible, put a thin square of latex rubber between your mouth and her privates. Latex squares (aka dental dams, latex barriers) are available from some sexual health clinics and dental suppliers. If you can't get hold of a shop-bought dam, you could try wrapping non-microwave cling film between your lover's legs – use a water-based lubricant (see page 113) on the side facing the clitoris. Or as a last resort, you could try using a cut-down and opened-out condom.

▶ Check before you bonk! If it looks as though all is not well with your partner's nether regions, perhaps because they've got a suspicious looking lump, bump or rash or an odd discharge coming from their penis/vagina, put your passion on hold and encourage your partner to get down to a sexual health clinic.

If either you or your partner has herpes simplex sores on the mouth (cold sores) or genitals, or any other type of sores/cuts/scratches, bleeding in the mouth or on the genitals, steer clear of kissing and oral sex until all is well again. (Take note: over-vigorous tooth brushing and flossing can make your gums bleed).

▶ If you want to practise anilingus (aka rimming, oral-anal sex, or licking your lover's anus), use a latex square. Anal germs which get inside the mouth can cause infections such as hepatitis A (see page 149).

▶ If you're female, try and wash your private parts and have a pee before vaginal sex and as soon as possible afterwards, too. This may help you avoid getting a very common sex-related infection called cystitis (see page 144). In fact, it makes sense for both partners to wash their private parts and dab them dry before sex. Both having clean hands is important, too.

▶ Tell your partner if you have an infection. He or she may have given you the infection without knowing and may also be re-infecting you without knowing.

▶ Wear cotton underwear and avoid wearing tights, tight-fitting trousers, cycle shorts etc. whenever possible. Hot, sweaty conditions may encourage bacteria and thrush to grow (see page 141).

▶ If you're female, always wipe your bottom from front to back to avoid transferring germs from your bottom to your pee hole or to your vagina.

▶ Avoid using lots of perfumed soaps, bath oils and foams which may irritate the delicate skin around your vagina/ penis. Vaginal deodorants are also best avoided as these can cause unnecessary soreness. Try not to wash your privates too much either. Staff at sexual health clinics see lots of people who have sore private parts due to over-washing.

Use a soapy hand to wash your private parts and bottom, and rinse thoroughly. Soapy flannels and sponges can harbour bacteria.

▶ Look after yourself. Eating healthily and getting enough rest and exercise will help your body ward off infections more easily.

Self-help for common infections and diseases

Here is a run-down of some sexually transmitted and genital infections and the steps you can take to help prevent yourself from getting them. (These are in addition to the general ones given above.) There are also some suggestions for self-help action you can take if you've had a particular infection once which has been diagnosed by a doctor and the symptoms reoccur. It's worth noting that many STIs and genital infections have similar symptoms, which makes it very difficult to diagnose yourself, so it's important to consult a doctor as soon as possible if you are in any doubt as to the cause of your symptoms.

Thrush
aka (also known as)

candidosis

candida albicans

Thrush is caused by a yeast called Candida albicans which usually lives quite harmlessly inside the body. Most of the time you don't know it's there. It's only when the yeast multiplies to cause an infection that you have a problem. Both sexes can get thrush. In girls it usually affects the vagina and vulva and in lads it can affect the penis.

Strictly speaking, thrush isn't a sexually transmitted infection, although it is possible to catch thrush from someone else during sex. Stress, antibiotics, the contraceptive pill, pregnancy, diabetes and wearing crotch-hugging, synthetic clothes can all make a person more likely to get thrush.

SYMPTOMS

▶ Itching around your genitals or anus which can drive you crazy.

▶ Soreness around your privates.

▶ Inflammation of the penis.

▶ Thick, white discharge from the vagina which usually looks a bit like cottage cheese.

▶ Pain on peeing and pain during vaginal sex.

> Men don't always get symptoms when they get thrush, so if a sexually active girl keeps on getting thrush, it's probably best if her partner sees a doctor too.

TEXTBOOK TREATMENT

The traditional treatment for thrush is a tablet or course of tablets which are inserted into the vagina (called pessaries), and some cream which is gently rubbed on to the vulva or penis. In recent years oral pills to treat thrush have come on to the market. These pills, like pessaries and cream, can be bought from a chemist's without a prescription, but it is worth getting your first attack of thrush diagnosed by a doctor before you try them. Once you are sure you have thrush, you will be able to recognize the symptoms in future and treat any recurrent attacks with one of these treatments yourself. (Remember, if you are in any doubt about whether or not you have thrush, see your doctor.)

PREVENTION

Following the advice on page 140 about wiping your bottom from front to back, wearing cotton underwear and taking care of your health will help prevent thrush. So too will avoiding perfumed soaps, vaginal deodorants and anything else likely to irritate your private parts, such as disinfectants.

If you're female, try to use sanitary pads rather than tampons when you have a period.

Thrush can flare up after a course of antibiotics. So if you are prescribed antibiotics and you are prone to thrush, tell your doctor.

> **FACT:** It is estimated that three out of four women will get thrush at some point in their lives.

SELF HELP

Once you've had thrush, you'll probably recognize it if you get it again.

If you can't get to your doctor or a pharmacist when symptoms reappear, stop using soap and try washing your privates in salt water from a basin or have a salt bath (1 teaspoon of table salt to 1 pint of water).

Don't scratch or rub the parts that hurt and don't have extra baths or showers. When you need to wash your privates, rinse them gently in cool water and pat them dry. Don't forget to change your towels and flannels often.

Avoid sex during an episode of thrush. If you don't,

you'll only aggravate your symptoms and if you don't use a condom you could pass the thrush on to your partner.

To soothe the itchiness caused by thrush, some women find it helps to put a tampon dipped in natural live yogurt into their vagina and/or to put natural live yogurt onto their vulva. Make sure you choose unpasteurized plain yogurt which contains lactobacilli. Sugar-laden fruit yogurts may taste delicious, but they won't do your nether regions any good at all.

Cystitis

Cystitis is an infection or inflammation of the bladder. It is a very common complaint amongst women, but men and boys can get it too.

Cystitis can be caused by germs from the bottom or anus getting into the urethra, or 'pee-tube', and up into the bladder. (Microscopic anal germs which weren't picked up by toilet paper after a bowel movement can get rubbed into the urethra during sex.) Cystitis can also be caused by bruising which can happen during vaginal sex.

> **FACT:** Cystitis is sometimes called the honeymoon disease because first-time vaginal sex (or vigorous vaginal sex) can bruise the urethra, which lies close to the inside of the vagina, and produce cystitis symptoms.

Like thrush, cystitis can occur without any sexual contact at all. Not drinking enough water-based drinks; holding on to your pee instead of going to the toilet; and drinking too much coffee, tea, alcohol or eating spicy foods (which can irritate the bladder) can all cause cystitis symptoms. So too can being allergic to certain perfumed soaps, bath products, vaginal deodorants, contraceptive gels and other chemical products which touch the urethral opening.

SYMPTOMS

▶ A burning sensation when you pee.

▶ A desperate desire to pee frequently, even though next to nothing comes out.

▶ A pain above the pubic bone.

▶ Sometimes blood or pus in your pee.

▶ Feverishness.

TEXTBOOK TREATMENT
Antibiotics are often prescribed to treat the germs causing cystitis.

PREVENTION
Try to drink a glass of water every few hours or so during the day. This will make you pee regularly and so flush germs out of your bladder.

Don't put off going for a pee when you need one.

If you are a girl, pee before and soon after sex and avoid putting anything in your vagina that might bruise or put pressure on your urethra. Using tampons and having sex in the rear entry position can both put pressure on a girl's urethra. Having penetrative sex when your vagina isn't well-lubricated can also irritate the vagina and so put pressure on the urethra.

Follow the advice given on pages 139-141 about wiping your bottom from front to back, washing your privates before sex and avoiding perfumed soaps, flannels and crotch-tight clothes.

Some women prone to cystitis drink a glass of cranberry juice every day to help prevent bacteria growing in their bladder.

SELF HELP

If you feel a bout of cystitis coming on and you can't get to your doctor straight away, collect some of your early morning pee in a clean, sterile jar – pee a little first and then collect the rest of your pee in the jar – and take it to the doctor as soon as you can. (Check with the surgery that they test urine samples, first.) While you're waiting to see the doctor...

Try to drink as much water as is sensibly possible. A glass of cold water at the start of an episode of cystitis and every 20 minutes after that for three hours usually helps speed up recovery.

You can buy short-term treatments for cystitis without a prescription from chemists. These treatments, which come in the form of sachets of powder which you dissolve in water, work by making your pee less acidic and so help stop any burning sensations. They also encourage you to drink more and so pee more frequently. As with all medicines, remember to read the leaflet that comes with the treatment.

Taking a couple of painkillers, avoiding strong tea, coffee, alcohol, spices and fruit juices, and not holding on to your pee should also help to reduce or stop cystitis symptoms.

If you have a bout of cystitis which lasts for more than 48 hours, or bouts which recur frequently or are accompanied by bleeding when peeing, severe stomach, groin or back-ache, or a temperature, fever or chill, you must see a doctor.

If you want more information about cystitis you could read Angela Kilmartin's book *Understanding Cystitis* published by Arrow Books.

Genital herpes simplex

Herpes simplex is caused by a virus. There are two common types of herpes; either can be the cause of cold sores or blisters on the lips, face and mouth and sores around the genitals and anus. If you have vaginal, anal or oral sex with anyone who is having an outbreak of herpes simplex, chances are you'll get it too.

SYMPTOMS

▶ Tingling or itching around the genitals; pain in the testicles.

▶ Sores on or around the genital area which develop into painful blisters.

▶ Other symptoms can include fever and general flu-like symptoms, pain on peeing, or discharge from the penis or vagina.

> Some people get an outbreak of herpes simplex once and once only. Others get repeated symptoms. The first episode, however, is usually the most painful.

TEXTBOOK TREATMENT

Although there are remedies which can ease the pain and shorten or prevent further outbreaks of herpes simplex, these are not essential as your body will get better by itself. However, all herpes viruses (and this includes chicken pox) have the ability to hide out in nerve ganglions and may reappear occasionally.

If you wanted to take a remedy, the drug Aciclovir, if started within the first day or two of an outbreak, can reduce pain and speed up healing in a primary outbreak, but it is of little help in recurrences.

PREVENTION

Follow the guidelines on pages 139-141. If your partner has a sore on their mouth or genitals avoid bringing any part of your body in touch with the sore/s ... and vice versa.

Always use a condom when having sex.

If you do touch a herpes simplex sore by mistake, wash your hands or the part of your body that it touched.

There are herpes vaccines being tested which may protect people unaffected by the disease in the future.

SELF HELP

The following tips may help relieve the discomfort of herpes simplex.

Wrap ice cubes in a hanky or flannel, put them in a plastic bag and hold them against the affected part.

You can also buy an anaesthetic ointment called Xylocaine from a chemist which will numb sore, itchy parts.

Have salt baths as these help relieve the pain and keep your privates clean.

Make sure your privates are exposed to the air as much as possible. When you have to wear underpants, make sure they are cotton and avoid tights and tight trousers.

If it hurts to pee in the usual way, pee in a basin of water, or in the shower or bath – making sure you clean it thoroughly afterwards.

Take a mild painkiller.

There are some essential oils, such as tea tree, eucalyptus or geranium, which may help if dabbed directly on to the sore before it has broken out. However, it is best to get advice from a qualified aromatherapist as to what's best in your case, as some find certain oils an irritant.

Eat well and get plenty of rest until the sores have gone.

> For more information about herpes simplex or viruses contact the Herpes Viruses Association, 41 North Road, London N7 9DB. Helpline 0171 609 9061.

Hepatitis

Hepatitis means inflammation of the liver. There are different types of hepatitis infection. Hepatitis B is a serious infection which can be passed on through body fluids such as blood, semen, saliva and pee. It is possible for a person carrying the hep B virus not to have any symptoms and pass on the infection without knowing they've got it.

SYMPTOMS

▶ Early symptoms include painful joints, loss of appetite and feeling very tired.

▶ Later symptoms include the skin turning yellowish and pee turning darkish brown.

TEXTBOOK TREATMENT

There is no effective treatment for this illness. People with hepatitis are usually advised to get plenty of rest and eat well.

PREVENTION

There is a hepatitis B vaccination which is available to people who are at high risk of catching the infection i.e. gay and bisexual men and intravenous drug users. If you are a member of this high risk group and want to have the vaccination talk to your doctor or call the National Hepatitis line on 0990 100 360.

Like hep B, hepatitis A can also cause serious illness. Risky sexual activities hep A-wise are those which involve the transfer of faeces, or shit, from one person's body into another. There is an injection available which protects against hep A, but it's hard to get if your risk is through sex. However, if you think you may be at risk, talk to your doctor/local sexual health clinic or call the National Hepatitis line.

Cervical cancer

Cervical cancer, or cancer of the cervix, is thought to be caused by a virus which can be passed on during sex. And the more partners you have, the more likely you are to meet the virus. To help protect yourself, always use a condom when you have vaginal sex and have a smear test every three years at your GP's or local clinic when you are aged 20 and older. A smear test can pick up cell changes in the cervix which could lead to cancer. As a rough rule there is no point in having a smear test before the age of 20 unless this is advised by a doctor because of your symptoms.

Chapter 8

sex

YOUNG, FREE AND ... PREGNANT!

Signs of pregnancy

The most usual early sign of pregnancy is a missed period. Feeling sick, throwing up, having tingly, tender breasts, feeling very tired and needing to go to the toilet a lot more than usual can also be early symptoms. A few women don't miss a period during pregnancy, but the 'periods' that they have while they are pregnant are usually lighter and shorter than their usual periods.

If you suspect you might be pregnant – perhaps because you've had unprotected sex and your period is late – you should have a pregnancy test done right away. Burying your head in the sand and ignoring the signs of pregnancy will not make it 'disappear'. If you are pregnant, it's best to find out as early as possible. That way you've got time to think very carefully about what you are going to do.

Pregnancy tests

Pregnancy tests usually involve testing a sample of your pee to see if it contains pregnancy hormones. You can have a free test done at a young person's clinic or Brook Advisory Centre, most family planning clinics, some doctor's surgeries and some sexual health clinics.

If you don't mind paying for a test you can ask a chemist or pharmacy to do one for you.

153

Alternatively you can buy a kit to use at home. Home pregnancy tests are handy because they let you find out your result in private. However, if you are worried about the result you might find it better to have your test done at a clinic because there you'll have a sympathetic doctor or counsellor to talk to if need be.

You can also get a test done by a pregnancy advisory service. Some pregnancy advisory services are anti-abortion, so if you think you are going to want an abortion it is best not to visit such organizations. Details of two large reputable organizations which won't try to pressurize you into doing anything you don't want to are given on pages 183-184.

Pregnancy tests can be negative, positive or uncertain. A positive result nearly always means that you are pregnant. A negative result usually means that you are not, but sometimes a test can read negative when you are in fact pregnant. One of the advantages of having your test done at a clinic is that if it is negative, you can have a chat with the clinic's health adviser to find out whether your test result could be wrong, and if it's not, why your period is late. If you do a home test which proves negative and your period still doesn't come, you should go to see your doctor or clinic.

Help! I'm pregnant ... what now?

Coping with an unplanned pregnancy on your own can be extremely stressful, which is why most young women find that it helps hugely to talk things through with their family and partner and/or someone from an advice service, such as a Brook Advisory Centre, a family planning clinic or a responsible pregnancy advisory service. Support services, such as Brook and the British Pregnancy Advisory Service, can help you work out whether you want to give birth and look after the baby yourself, perhaps in conjunction with your partner and/or your family; give birth and put the baby up for adoption or fostering; or have an abortion, i.e. have your pregnancy terminated by a doctor.

It is also a good idea for the lad involved in an unplanned pregnancy to talk about how he feels with his partner and family and/or someone from an advice service.

Having a baby

Having a baby to love can be unbelievably blissful, but looking after one is hard work and costly so it makes sense to think long and hard before choosing to raise a child. If after careful thought and talking things through with the baby's father, your family and/or a support service, you do decide to keep your baby, go and see your doctor as soon as you can, so that s/he can arrange for you to receive ante-natal, i.e. before-birth, care throughout your pregnancy. If you don't want to see your own GP, you can register with another local one for the course of your pregnancy. Look under 'Doctors' in the Yellow Pages and choose one. Ring the receptionist and explain that you want to register for family planning/maternity purposes. If you are under 16, check with the receptionist that the doctor you have chosen will treat what you tell him/her in confidence.

There are a number of excellent organizations which provide information and advice for mums-to-be and single mums and dads. See pages 183-186 for more details. The midwife who sees a young mum during her pregnancy may also have information about local groups and organizations which can provide support and information.

When I first found out I was pregnant, it was a shock. I thought, 'My God, how am I going to tell my parents?' I kept it from them for several days, and it made me really tense. In the end, I had to take my mum out into the garden; I couldn't talk to her with my dad there. She was OK, really; my dad's reaction was different. He was shocked: what would I do, how would I cope – but

Mum reassured him.

I'd been on the pill, but I came off it: I found it made me feel ill. I wasn't with Stewart at the time – we'd split up a few weeks before; he'd just come round and it was a kind of one-off. I went to the clinic for a test when I first suspected and it came up negative. Then a month later I went again, and it was positive – so then I was eight weeks pregnant.

Abortion? I would never even have considered it. I think some girls see abortion as a form of contraception, and I think that's wrong. And it doesn't take the boy's point of view into account. I don't believe in it. I think if you're old enough to be in a sexual relationship, you're old enough to deal with the consequences.

Stewart said he'd stick by me, and in fact we're back together again now. He was with me in the hospital when she was born, just him and the midwife. I didn't want anyone else; he bathed my face with water, and rubbed my back – he was so chuffed when she was born: you should have seen his face! It was quite a relaxed labour, only five and a half hours.

The best times are watching her grow up, things like seeing her first smile, and her cooing at you.

The worst times are when she's really, really whingeing and won't go to sleep; she's teething at the moment and can be really grizzly sometimes. Sleep problems are the worst.

My parents helped me a lot: they were really supportive. Financial support is important. They paid for the pram, and helped decorate her room. They do still help quite a lot.

In some ways, yes, I wish I'd waited. After college, I'd wanted to go on to university, or to become a social worker. All that's got to wait now. Sometimes I see my friends, and they go out clubbing twice a week, or say, 'Let's go to the pub' – and I can't, I have to think about getting a babysitter, and about the money side of *things. I can take her to family things; but I can't go out clubbing as I used to. It definitely limits your social life. You have to go without: you don't have as much money for clothes, there are so many things you need for the baby – and anyway, there's no point in wearing decent clothes when they'll only get puked on or messy. It takes twice as long to get ready to go out – everything has to be planned, getting all the baby things together even for a few hours. But you can't plan anything three weeks ahead – you've got to take each day as it comes, got to realize the baby comes first.*

Looking at her, I'd never not have done it; it was a mistake, but in a way a mistake I'm glad I made. It's certainly made me think. I've grown up quite a lot: you have to take responsibility for someone else. It's really a worry sometimes, if you're on your own, and they're ill. If they're really screaming, and you can't tell where it hurts, it's awful.

At school, they really don't tell you enough about it, not in detail. It's not enough just to practise putting a condom on a carrot! I've got a friend who's 17, her baby is six months old; she used a condom and it split. They should tell you about things like that. And about pregnancy, and how you can get heartburn and things: I was quite lucky, I only got it at the end. How you can't bend down and touch your toes; and how you need to get up in the night to go to the toilet. Mind you, that gets you used to getting up in the night to feed the baby.

What I'd say to other young people is, make sure you take precautions. If you do get pregnant, don't hide it. Make sure you tell your parents: you need all the support you can get. It certainly changes your life. You can't see your friends as much, you miss out on social life. People don't realize the time it takes: they think babies just lie there doing nothing, but they're so demanding, you're on the go all the time, and you're

always washing clothes! By the end of the day you're worn out. The only time I have to myself is in the evening, when she's asleep; then I have to cook, and we can spend some time together. But you don't have much time for your relationship, even that has to go on hold. You have to put your own life on hold.
(Kerry, 19)

Single dads

> **FACT:** A childbirth instructor in the USA has invented an artificial pregnant belly which allows the person wearing it (perhaps fathers-to-be, or young girls) to feel some of the symptoms of pregnancy such as heartburn, pressure on the bladder and a baby's kicking.

A single dad has no automatic rights over his child. So, if you are a single dad and want to see your child regularly and take responsibility for supporting him/her against the wishes of the child's mother, you will have to apply to the law courts for parental responsibility. For advice on your rights as a single dad, contact a solicitor or the Citizens Advice Bureau and/or the voluntary self-help society, Families Need Fathers (see page 185 for details).

'*My girlfriend, Natasha, was 17 and I was nearly 20. We'd been together for two years when we found she was pregnant. At first we were shocked, but we quickly got used to the idea and were quite chuffed. Natasha was happy with the idea of being a mum, and she was OK about leaving college; we were already living in a flat together by then. Our families were pretty supportive.*

I was overjoyed to be a father – it's the most amazing feeling that, between you, you've created another life. I was there at her birth: it was a great experience, and I felt really close to both of them. It was a trouble-free birth, Rosie was a lovely baby, and everything seemed to be fine.

I had taken out a couple of bank loans to cover a car, and other bills, and I was working hard to pay off my debts. Even though our families helped when they could, we were pretty skint. After a time, tensions started to build up: Natasha was getting restless, and I think beginning to regret having given up college and the chance of a career. I think she felt trapped. We moved to a council house soon after Rosie was born: there was more space, but it was more expensive, so I took on a load of overtime.

Natasha started to leave Rosie with her mum and go out with friends while I was working. We began to argue more and more, and in the end she moved back in with her parents.

Now we've been separated for about a year. I'm still working to pay off my debts and all the money the Child Support Agency demands I pay to her. I'd do anything to help Rosie: I don't begrudge the money for her – I'd like to be able to save some up for her when she's older, but I haven't enough at the moment. It's hard, though, because I'm not welcome at Natasha's parents' house, and I don't get to see Rosie very often.

> *I'm trying to work something out so we can at least be friends enough to talk sensibly, and plan something together for Rosie's future.*
> *(Jonathan, 22)*

Adoption

Adoption means having your baby and then giving it to new parents to bring up as their own child. Fostering means giving birth to your baby and then allowing it to be looked after by a family or a home, until you are able to look after it yourself.

If you think that you might want to have your baby adopted, contact your local authority's Social Services Department (Social Work Department in Scotland) or an approved adoption agency and arrange to talk to a social worker about adoption. Many hospitals employ social workers who work with maternity clinics and could also advise you. The British Agencies for Adoption and Fostering (BAAF) produces a book which lists local authority and approved adoption agencies. See page 185 for their address.

Making the decision whether or not to have your baby adopted is one of the most important decisions you'll ever have to make, so it's worth getting as much advice as you can before you make up your mind. If, after talking things through, you decide that adoption is the best option for you and your baby, a social worker will ask you some questions about yourself and your family and collect your views on what kind of family you want your child to grow up in. Although this marks the beginning of preparations for the adoption, nothing will be arranged definitely until after the birth of your child. This means you can change your mind during your pregnancy if you want to. In fact, because adoption is such a big step for a mother to take, the law says that there must be a delay of at least six weeks after the birth before the mother signs a formal document, giving her agreement to the adoption. So, if you change your mind before you sign this document, you will probably be able to keep your baby even if it has already gone to live with its adoptive parents. It is only once the adoption order has been granted by a court of law that you no longer have any legal relationship with your child.

Adoption and dads

If a dad is not married to the mother of his child, and has no parental responsibility for that child, he doesn't have to give his permission for an adoption to take place. By law, social workers have to try and contact the father of a child being put up for adoption in order to get his views on the matter (he may want to try and adopt his child himself) and to try and get some details about him that the child might want to know when it is grown up. It is usually in the baby's best interests that this contact is made with the natural father.

Abortion
aka (also known as)

termination

termination of pregnancy

FACT: In 1988 1,590,800 abortions were performed in the USA. That works out at around 182 abortions every hour.

Deciding whether or not to have an abortion is an extremely important decision to make and one which should never be rushed into. This is why many young women considering abortion talk the matter over with those they are close to as well as getting expert advice.

If, after careful consideration, you decide that abortion is the best option for you, you need to act quickly. If you live in England, Scotland or Wales, visit your own GP, another GP (see 'Having the Baby' above), a family planning clinic or a Brook Advisory Centre straight away. Early abortions are easier to get and far less complicated medically than late ones, so the sooner you have the abortion, the better.

You don't have an automatic right to an abortion (see page 170 for more details), but many women who seek abortions get them done free on the National Health Service (NHS). Those who are unwilling or unable to get an NHS abortion often go to a private clinic where they have to pay to have their pregnancy ended. You'll find details of two charitable organizations offering private abortions on pages 183-184.

If you live in Northern Ireland you won't be able to get a free abortion because abortions are illegal there. You could, however, contact the Family Planning Association or the Ulster Pregnancy Advisory Service and make an appointment to see someone. Both organizations can arrange for women to have private abortions in England.

For more details about abortion and the law, turn to page 170.

> **FACT:** There are 65 countries in the world where abortion is illegal and punishable by imprisonment.

Abortion procedures

If you are less than nine weeks pregnant i.e. it's less than nine weeks since your last period, and you are seeking an abortion, you may be given the abortion pill (aka Mifegyne (RU 486)), which should trigger a miscarriage. If you choose this type of abortion and two doctors agree that it is suitable for you, you will be given a dose of pills which will interrupt the natural growth of your pregnancy. A couple of days later, you will be admitted to a bed in the clinic or hospital; you will be given a pessary to insert into your vagina which will make your uterus expel the embryo from your body. This process, which takes about six hours, is like having a heavy period and can be painful.

> **FACT**: Up until the eighth week of pregnancy the developing ball of cells inside a woman's uterus is called an embryo. After that it is called a foetus.

If you are between six and 15 weeks pregnant you will probably undergo a quick, fairly straightforward operation called a vacuum aspiration which involves gently opening the neck of your uterus and removing the contents. You will be given an anaesthetic – either local or light general – and recovery is usually made within two to three hours.

Abortions performed after the 15th week of pregnancy are more complicated to perform than early surgical abortions and tend to be more upsetting for everyone involved.

After an abortion

Having an abortion may leave you feeling relieved. But it can also leave you feeling sad, guilty, depressed or even worried that you don't feel sad, guilty or depressed enough. If you are able to talk to others before the abortion and work through your feelings, you are less likely to feel deeply depressed after the operation. If you do feel depressed, though, you may find it helpful to talk to a counsellor or join a post-abortion support group.

Abortion myths

The only way to have a safe abortion is to have a legal abortion. Idiots may tell you that you can bring on an abortion yourself by drinking lots of gin, having a hot bath, jumping from a height, falling down the stairs, sticking something sharp into your uterus, squirting fluids up your vagina, or riding a bicycle over a bumpy field. Not only do these methods not work, some of them are mind-bogglingly dangerous.

Chapter 9

sex

SEX AND THE LAW

There are a number of laws in England, Wales, Scotland and Northern Ireland concerning marriage and sex. Here's a rundown of the main ones and some other useful information.

The age of consent for heterosexuals

The age of consent is the minimum age a person has to be to have sex lawfully. In Scotland, England and Wales the age of consent is 16. In Northern Ireland it is 17.

If a lad has sex with a girl who is under the age of consent, no matter how willing she is, he, not she, is the one guilty of breaking the law.

A girl or woman cannot be prosecuted for unlawful sexual intercourse with a man or boy. However, if the boy is under 16 she could be charged with indecent assault.

Anal intercourse between heterosexuals is only legal if both people involved are willing and aged 18 or over. Anal intercourse with someone under the age of 16 carries a maximum penalty of life imprisonment.

The age of consent for homosexuals

The age of consent for gay men is 18 years throughout the United Kingdom at the time of writing, and 21 in the Isle of Man.

There is no law against two women having sex at any age. However, if an older woman was caught having sex with an under-age girl she could be charged with indecent assault.

FACT: Lesbian relationships have never been illegal. This is because law makers in Queen Victoria's time believed that women were incapable of being assertive sexually. As a result, sexy goings-on between two girls were just not thought possible.

Homosexual relationships between members of the armed forces or crew members of merchant navy ships are not illegal, but if they are discovered they can lead to sacking from the services.

Marriage

In England, Wales, Scotland and Northern Ireland the minimum age for marriage is 16 years. In England, Wales and Northern Ireland, anyone under 18 (i.e. 16 and 17 year olds) needs their parents' consent before they can get married. In Scotland parental permission is not necessary.

> **FACT**: Any girl living in ancient Rome who was not married by the time she was 18 had good reason to worry about being left on the shelf. Back then, many girls were married by the time they were 12 years old.

Contraception
Over 16s

Anyone over 16 can consent to medical treatment in their own right and can be given free contraceptive advice and supplies by their own doctor, another GP or a family planning clinic without their parents' or guardians' knowledge or permission.

Under 16s

Doctors can give confidential contraceptive supplies to people under 16 in certain circumstances. Doctors have strict guidelines to follow and one of these says that a doctor must try and persuade an under-age person to tell their parents/guardians of any contraceptive advice or supplies given. If the young person won't agree to this, the doctor must then decide whether s/he thinks that:

A the young person is mature enough to fully understand the choices involved and the benefits and risks of any contraceptives given;

B the young person would suffer mentally or physically if not given contraceptive advice or supplies;

C it is in the young person's best medical interests to be given contraceptive advice or supplies without parental knowledge or consent;

D the young person is likely to start or to continue having sex without contraception.

If the doctor is convinced that it is in the young person's best interests to be given contraceptives without parental consent, s/he will do just that. Even if the doctor thinks that the young person is too immature to be given contraceptives, it is unlikely that s/he will tell the young person's parents or guardians about the meeting. Doctors are advised to build up trusting relationships with their patients and to break that trust only in exceptional circumstances.

If you are under-age and want advice about contraception but don't want to see your own GP, you can always register with another, or visit your local young person's clinic, or Brook Advisory Centre where your visit is guaranteed to be confidential. If you do set off in search of another GP, explain to his/her receptionist that you want to register with a doctor for family planning purposes only, and check that the doctor can offer you a full range of contraceptive methods confidentially. If the receptionist is unhelpful, go elsewhere. Lists of doctors can be found in libraries, post offices, advice centres and health authorities or Health and Social Services Boards. Doctors who offer contraceptive advice have the letter 'C' after their names.

Abortion

Abortion is legal in England, Scotland and Wales if two registered doctors agree that:

a) the woman is no more than 24 weeks pregnant and that carrying on with the pregnancy is likely to involve more risk to her physical or mental health than having an abortion (doctors can take into account the woman's social circumstances);

b) the woman is no more than 24 weeks pregnant and that carrying on with the pregnancy is likely to involve more risk to the physical or mental health of any children she already has than if she had an abortion;

c) the pregnant woman's physical or mental health will be seriously and permanently damaged if she doesn't have the abortion;

d) the pregnancy puts the woman's life at risk;

e) there is a big risk that the child would be born seriously handicapped, either mentally or physically.

The law on abortion can be read in different ways. Doctors

who believe that a woman has the right to choose whether she has a baby or not, tend to allow abortions on the basis that an early abortion is likely to be safer than giving birth normally and therefore is in line with the abortion law.

In England, Scotland and Wales a girl under the age of 16 is very unlikely to be given an abortion without the consent of one of her parents/guardians.

No woman can be made to have an abortion, whatever her age.

Behaving sexually in public

If a man deliberately exposes his private parts to a woman or girl with the intention of insulting her he is committing an offence and can be fined or sent to prison.

If a woman exposes her body in public in an indecent way she can be charged with indecent exposure too.

Any couple found having sex or doing very sexual things in a public place can be charged with outraging public decency.

Prostitution

A prostitute (aka whore, tart, hooker) is someone who has sex in return for payment. Prostitution itself is not illegal, but what is illegal is trying to pick up 'customers', either through advertisements or standing on street corners, and pimping i.e. living off money earned through prostitution.

Men who drive around slowly looking for prostitutes on street corners to have sex with are called kerb crawlers. Kerb crawling became an offence in 1985.

> **FACT:** Areas of a city where prostitutes gather and work are often called red light districts. The association between prostitutes and the colour red dates back to medieval times when it became law in France for brothels, or whore-houses, to display a red lantern.

Rape

Rape happens when someone forces another person, male or female, to have vaginal or anal sex against their will. Even if the person being raped is unable to put up a fight, either because they are too scared or drunk or even asleep, their attacker can still be found guilty of rape. Rape is a very serious offence and the penalty is a hefty prison sentence.

Indecent assault is when one person touches another person in a very sexual way without any kind of permission. This too is illegal, as is forcing someone to perform oral sex when they don't want to.

When I was fourteen I had a horrible experience that I'll remember for the rest of my life. I was raped.

It was Saturday night and I was out with my best friend, who I've known for ages and trusted – we'd shared all sorts of secrets and experiences together. We'd spent the day watching our team play football, and we decided to go to the pub for a drink. Then we met up with these two blokes: one of them knew my friend, and I knew the other one's brothers from school. They asked if we wanted to go for a drive, so we got into the car and drove off, my friend in the front with the one she knew, and me in the back with the other.

I didn't recognize any of the roads after a bit, and didn't know where we were going. Eventually we stopped near some woods, but I'd no idea where we were. The conversation centred mainly around sex, and I felt very uncomfortable. After a bit he started touching me in between my legs, right up to the top, and he was kissing me. I didn't mind the kissing, just for a bit of fun, but then he undid the buttons on my trousers – and I started to feel really uneasy and frightened.

He kept whispering things in my ear, like 'Come on, let's do it,' and I said 'No!' But then he made it quite clear to the pair in the front what he wanted to do, and they joined in the argument. My friend was saying, 'You might as well, no-one will know, just have fun, go on.' I was really frightened, and also he hadn't any contraception – not that I'd have wanted to do it if he had.

Then he pushed me down on to the back seat and pulled my trousers and knickers down and raped me. I was crying, but he didn't care – no-one cared. I seemed to just shut myself off from it all, kind of blocked it all out. After I got home, I felt so horrible that I washed and bathed twice a day and more, and I had all my hair cut off because it felt so dirty.

I couldn't sleep, and I felt I couldn't tell my mum what had happened because I was afraid that she'd be angry and think it was my fault. But like all mums doing their job she noticed something was wrong, and in the end she asked me why I was so unhappy. I just broke down and told her everything. She was so understanding, her heart was full of anger at the bloke and sympathy for me.

A few days passed and I kept pleading with her not to go to the police, but she felt there was nothing else she could do. My school work was going downhill, and I was so tired I didn't have the energy to do anything. I had nightmares for three months, all of the same thing.

In the end the police came and took a statement, and he was arrested and charged. It hasn't been easy since, and I'm not friends with that girl any longer, but I had a lot of help from Victim Support, and I'm now starting to lead my life the way I want to again. I have a boyfriend now who really cares and who I trust. I think that trust is the main thing that I need to feel safe again.

(Michelle, 15)

What to do if you've been raped

Rape is a hideous crime. If ever you are in the horrible position of just having been raped, here are some practical tips you might find helpful.

> ▶ Get some medical attention as soon as possible, even if you haven't got any visible injuries. Your attacker may have given you a sexually transmitted infection.
>
> ▶ Tell someone what has happened as soon as you can, if you can, so that you have a witness to your distress, if needed.
>
> ▶ If you decide to report the rape to the police (which you should do if you want your attacker caught and prevented from abusing anyone else), don't wash, shower or bathe straight after the attack. You may wash away crucial clues that could lead the police to your attacker. Don't change your clothes either. Go to the police as soon as you can, as you are. Your crumpled clothes etc. will back up your story. Take some spare clothes with you if you can just in case the police want to hang on to yours for evidence.
>
> ▶ Contact a supportive friend or relative or someone at a local rape crisis centre to give you help and comfort during your visit to the police station and/or medical check-up. You can always ring someone from the police station.
>
> ▶ Don't, whatever you do, think that you are responsible for being raped. No one 'asks' to be or deserves to be raped.

> ◗ To help yourself get over the rape, try and talk to someone about your feelings. There are details of helpful organizations at the back of this book.

Be safe

Although a large number of rapes and sexual assaults are not committed by strangers, it makes sense to avoid dodgy places, such as deserted paths, and dicey situations, such as hitching a ride alone with a stranger. It also makes sense if you're planning a night out on the town to think about how you are going to get home. If there isn't any public transport available, take some money for a taxi or a phone call home, or arrange to walk back home with a friend. If you have to walk home alone, walk confidently along busy well-lit streets and be aware of what is going on around you. Wear shoes and clothes you can run in and have your keys ready in your hand when you reach your door. All this applies to both sexes since both sexes can be assaulted and raped. To be on the safe side, you could learn self-defence or carry a personal alarm with you. These small gadgets, which are fairly cheap to buy, let out a deafening noise.

Sexual abuse

It is a criminal offence to have sex with someone in your immediate family e.g. your father, mother, grandmother, grandfather, brother, half-brother, sister, half-sister, uncle or aunt. This type of sex is called incest.

What to do if you're being sexually abused by an adult

Most parents, grandparents, uncles, aunts, teachers and other adults are normal, well-adjusted people who would never dream of taking advantage of the power or authority they have over a young person. However, there is a small number of people who are not so responsible and who use their authority to force or persuade young people into sexual acts or situations. If you have been or are being sexually abused in any way – perhaps you are being made to look at pornography or you are being touched sexually or forced to have sex against your will – you should tell someone you trust or telephone a helpline such as ChildLine (see page 191 for details of this organization and others). No matter what your abuser may tell you they, not you, are to blame for the abuse. Being forced to have sex with an adult you should be able to trust can be a very damaging experience, and you need to talk to someone who can be trusted about your feelings to help you get over the abuse.

FACT: ChildLine is a free national telephone helpline for young people in trouble or danger. In 1995/96, 7,856 young people contacted ChildLine about sexual abuse.

sex
speak

Here's a selection of words and terms to do with sex, most of which you won't have come across in this book.

(A) APHRODISIAC Something which you eat or drink or smell which is said to make you feel sexually excited or which is supposedly meant to make others feel sexually excited by you. Oysters are said to be an aphrodisiac.

(B) BREWER'S DROOP Slang term for a lad's inability to get an erection because he's had too much alcohol to drink.

(C) CELIBATE Someone who has chosen to live without sex.

(D) DILDO Penis-shaped sex toy which can be put inside a vagina or anus.

(F) FETISHIST Someone who is turned on sexually by seeing or touching something which is not necessarily sexual in itself, e.g. shiny black stiletto boots or skimpy white knickers.

FLASHER Someone who likes exposing their private parts in public.

FOREPLAY All the sexual things you do in the lead-up to penetrative sex.

(G) GENITAL WARTS A common sexually transmitted infection.

GONORRHOEA A type of sexually transmitted infection.

(I) **IMPOTENCE** An inability to get or hold an erection.

(K) **KAMA SUTRA** A book written by a fifth-century Hindu which describes traditional modes of courtship and lots of different sexual positions.

(L) **LOVE BITE** A bruise-like mark left on the skin after someone has sucked it really hard.

(M) **MARITAL AIDS** Sex toys such as dildos and vibrators.

(N) **NECKING** Sometimes described as light petting: sex play which involves things like kissing and touching your lover's body through their clothes, but doesn't include sexual intercourse.

(O) **ORGY** Group sex

(P) **PAEDOPHILE** Someone who is sexually attracted to children.

PETTING Sex play which includes anything except sexual intercourse, or penetrative sex. Also known as making out, heavy petting, getting off.

PORNOGRAPHY The name given to sexually-explicit pictures, photographs, films and writing which are produced to entertain and titillate.

(S) **SIXTY-NINE** The head-to-toe position a couple adopt when they want to lick and suck each other's private parts at the same time.

TRANSVESTITE Someone who likes wearing clothes usually associated with the opposite sex. Transvestites are not necessarily homosexual.

TRANSSEXUAL Someone who feels that they were born the wrong sex.

 VIBRATOR A penis-shaped, battery-operated sex toy which vibrates very quickly. Some women enjoy the feelings of the vibrator held against the clitoris.

Answers to quiz (page 13)

1. a)
2. b)
3. c)
4. a)
5. a), b) and c)
6. c)
7. b)
8. a)
9. a)
10. b)
11. a)
12. b)

sex
HELPFUL CONTACTS

Here is an assortment of addresses and phone numbers which you may at some time find useful.

Brook Advisory Centres
165 Grays Inn Road
London WC1X 8UD
0171 713 9000 (line open Mon-Fri 9am-5pm)

There are Brook Centres all across the UK.
The following Brook helplines provide 24-hour recorded information:

Emergency contraception **0171 617 0801**

Missed a period? **0171 617 0802**

Abortion **0171 617 0803**

Starting contraception **0171 617 0804**

Pregnant and unsure? **0171 617 0805**

Visiting a Brook Centre **0171 617 0806**

Sexually transmitted infections **0171 617 0807**

Brook Centres provide free, confidential contraceptive advice and supplies and help with sex-related or sexual health problems to young people under 25, even those under 16. Ring the 713 9000 number if you want details of your nearest Brook Centre or young people's sexual health clinic.

Family Planning Association (FPA)
FPA UK: 2-12 Pentonville Road
London N1 9FP
Contraceptive Education Service Helpline:
0171 837 4044 (line open Mon-Fri 9am-7pm)

FPA Wales
4 Museum Place
Cardiff CF1 3BG
01222 342766 (line open Mon-Fri 9am-5pm)

FPA Scotland
Unit 10, Firhill Business Centre
76 Firhill Road
Glasgow G20 7BA
0141 576 5088 (line open Mon-Fri 9am-5pm)

FPA Northern Ireland
113 University Street
Belfast BT7 1HP
01232 325488 (line open Mon-Fri 9am-5pm)

Call the FPA to find your nearest family planning or sexual health clinic, or for confidential information and advice about contraception and sexual health. They can send you a leaflet about whichever method of contraception you want to know more about. Remember to enclose a stamped self-addressed envelope if you write.

British Pregnancy Advisory Service (BPAS)
Head Office
Austy Manor
Wootton Wawen
Solihull
West Midlands B95 6BX
01564 793 225
BPAS Action Line: **0345 304030**

BPAS, which has branches throughout Britain, offers confidential information, counselling and treatment linked with contraception and pregnancy, including abortion. The BPAS action line is a local-telephone-rate phone line for women with unplanned pregnancies who want to make an

183

appointment with a BPAS member of staff to talk about the options open to them. The line is open 7 days a week Mon-Fri 8am-8pm; Sat 8.30am-6pm; Sun 9.30am-3.30pm.

Marie Stopes International
Head Office
Marie Stopes House
108 Whitfield Street
London W1P 6BE
National Helpline: **0800 716 390**
(line open Mon-Sat)

Marie Stopes International is a private charity with centres throughout the UK. It helps women with unplanned pregnancy and provides pregnancy testing, emergency contraception, counselling, abortions up to 24 weeks and contraceptive advice.

Life
62 Courthouse Road
London N12
0181 446 3514

Life can provide practical and emotional support for pregnant women as an alternative to abortion.

National Childbirth Trust
Alexandra House
Oldham Terrace
London W3 6NH
0181 992 8637

This organization can offer advice to pregnant girls about pregnancy, childbirth, breast-feeding etc.

British Agencies for Adoption and Fostering
Skyline House
200 Union Street
London SE1 OLX
0171 593 2000

BAAF produces books and leaflets about adoption and fostering including a useful information pack and a cheap, helpful leaflet called *Single, pregnant and thinking about adoption.* Remember to enclose a stamped self-addressed envelope if you want a leaflet.

National Council for One Parent Families
255 Kentish Town Road
London NW5 2LX
0171 267 1361

This organization provides information and advice for single, pregnant women and single mums and dads. It also campaigns on their behalf.

Families Need Fathers
134 Curtain Road
London EC2A 3AR
0171 613 5060
Information line: **0181 886 0970**

FNF is a society for children's rights which can provide invaluable advice and support on children's issues for dads, or mums, who are divorced, separated and unmarried. The society can help children trace their absentee fathers, too.

Gingerbread
England/Wales: **0171 336 8183**
Scotland: **0141 353 0953**
Northern Ireland: **01232 234 568**

The Gingerbread organizations run a nationwide network of self-help groups which offer friendship, support and practical advice to single parents. The different organizations also provide a variety of other support services. To find your nearest group or to get more details of the support services on offer, call one of the numbers above during office hours.

Youth Access
1a Taylors Yard
67 Alderbrook Road
London SW12 8AD
0181 772 9900

If you want to talk over a problem with a trained counsellor, Youth Access can try and refer you to someone in your area. Their service is free and confidential and is mainly aimed at people aged 14-25 years old. If you write, remember to enclose a stamped self-addressed envelope.

London Lesbian and Gay Switchboard
0171 837 7324 (line open 24 hours a day, 7 days a week)

LLGS offers information and help to anyone who is or thinks they may be lesbian, gay, bisexual, transsexual or a transvestite. It also offers advice about HIV/AIDS and safer sex. The telephone line, which is a national helpline, is often busy, so be patient!

Lothian Gay and Lesbian Switchboard
PO Box 169
Edinburgh EH1 3UU
Gay and lesbian helpline: **0131 556 4049**
Lesbian helpline: **0131 557 0751**
Administration and fax: **0131 556 8997**

In addition to providing the above helplines, Lothian Gay and Lesbian Switchboard also produces an excellent booklet called *Coming Out* which is well worth reading before deciding to come out to family or friends.

For a copy of this booklet send 60p and a stamped self-addressed envelope to the above address.

Lesbian Youth Support Information Service (LYSIS)
PO Box 8
Todmorden
Lancashire OL14 5TZ
Helpline: **01706 817235** (line open Mon-Thurs 9am-1pm and Wednesday 7pm-9pm)

LYSIS offers information and support to lesbians and produces a useful pack called the Young Lesbian Coming Out pack and a booklet called *i think i might be a lesbian ... now what do i do?*

Albert Kennedy Trust
Unit 305A, Hatton Square
16-16A Baldwin Gardens
London EC1N 7RJ
0171 831 6562
and
23 New Mount Street
Manchester M4 4DE
0161 953 4059

This organization provides supportive lodgings and on-going structured support in the London and Manchester areas for young people who are in danger of being made homeless because of their sexuality. The Trust works with young people who are under 20.

Lesbian and Gay Christian Movement
Oxford House
Derbyshire Street
London E2 6HG
0171 739 1249
Helpline: **0171 739 8134**

This organization offers help to gays and lesbians who are Christians.

Jewish Lesbian/Gay Helpline
0171 706 3123

The Naz Project London
Palingswick House
241 King Street
London W6 9LP
0181 741 1879

The Naz Project offers help on a range of sexual issues, including HIV/AIDS, to straight and gay people from the South Asian, Middle Eastern and North African communities.

SHAKI (South Asian Lesbian and Gay Network)
86 Caledonian Road
London N1
0171 837 3337

Blackliners
Unit 46 Eurolink Business Centre
49 Effra Road,
London SW2 1BZ
Helpline: **0171 738 5274** (line open Mon-Fri 9.30am-5.30am)

Blackliners offers, amongst other things, information and advice about HIV/AIDS and safer sex to people who are of African, Caribbean or Asian descent.

FFLAG (Families and Friends of Lesbians and Gays)
3 Hillside
West Boldon
South Tyneside NE36 OJG
0191 537 4691

FFLAG runs a network of local groups for parents of gay children.

Acceptance
64 Holmside Avenue
Sheerness
Kent, ME12 3EY
Helpline: **01795 661463** (line open Tues-Fri 7pm-9pm)

Acceptance offers help and support for parents of lesbians and gays.

Parents' Friend
Helpline: **0113 267 4627** (line open weekdays 8pm-10pm)

Parents' Friend offers help to young lesbians and gays who want to help their parents come to terms with their children's sexuality.

SPOD
Tel: **0171 607 8851** (line open Mon-Fri 9am-5pm)

SPOD offers help and information about sex and relationships to anyone who is disabled or who has a disabled partner.

The Terrence Higgins Trust
52-54 Grays Inn Road
London WC1X 8JU
Helpline: **0171 242 1010** (12pm-10pm)

The THT offers practical support, help, counselling and advice for anyone with or concerned about HIV/AIDS.

National Advisory Service on Aids
National Aids Helpline: **0800 567123**
National Aids Helpline (minicom): **0800 0521 361**
National Aids leaflet line: **0800 555 777**

Phone the helpline if you want confidential help or advice on HIV/AIDS and the leaflet line if you want to be sent leaflets about HIV/AIDS. The national lines are open 24 hours a day and calls to them are free from anywhere in England or Northern Ireland.

Gay Men Fighting AIDS
0171 738 6872 (9am-5pm)

Call this number if you want to be sent information about HIV/AIDS and safer sex for gay men.

The National Association for Pre-Menstrual Syndrome
PO Box 72
Sevenoaks
Kent TN13 1XQ
Information line for details of the day's helplines:
01732 741709

NAPS provides help, information and support to women and their families who suffer from the misery of PMS.

ChildLine
Freepost 1111
London N1 OBR
Helpline: **0800 1111** (line open 24 hours a day,
7 days a week)

ChildLine is the free, national telephone helpline for children and young people in trouble or danger. It can offer confidential help to any child with any problem. Calls are free to children calling 0800 1111 from anywhere in the country or children can write to the freepost address above.

Rape Crisis Centre
0171 837 1600 (line open weekdays 6pm-10pm and weekends 10am-10pm)

Offers information and advice to women and girls who have been raped or sexually assaulted either recently or in the past.

Survivors
PO Box 2470
London SW9 9ZP
Helpline: **0171 833 3737** (line open Mon, Tues, Weds 7pm-10pm)

Offers information and advice to men and boys who have been raped or sexually abused.